Two Woodwind Quintets

Recent Researches in Music

A-R Editions publishes seven series of critical editions, spanning the history of Western music, American music, and oral traditions.

Recent Researches in the Music of the Middle Ages and Early Renaissance
   Charles M. Atkinson, general editor

Recent Researches in the Music of the Renaissance
   James Haar, general editor

Recent Researches in the Music of the Baroque Era
   Christoph Wolff, general editor

Recent Researches in the Music of the Classical Era
   Neal Zaslaw, general editor

Recent Researches in the Music of the Nineteenth and Early Twentieth Centuries
   Rufus Hallmark, general editor

Recent Researches in American Music
   John M. Graziano, general editor

Recent Researches in the Oral Traditions of Music
   Philip V. Bohlman, general editor

Each edition in *Recent Researches* is devoted to works by a single composer or to a single genre. The content is chosen for its high quality and historical importance and is edited according to the scholarly standards that govern the making of all reliable editions.

For information on establishing a standing order to any of our series, or for editorial guidelines on submitting proposals, please contact:

A-R Editions, Inc.
Middleton, Wisconsin

800 736-0070 (U.S. book orders)
608 836-9000 (phone)
608 831-8200 (fax)
http://www.areditions.com

Recent Researches in the Music of the Nineteenth and Early Twentieth Centuries, 39

Franz Lachner

Two Woodwind Quintets

Edited by L. Jonathan Saylor

A-R Editions, Inc.
Middleton, Wisconsin

For my parents

Performance parts are available from the publisher.

A-R Editions, Inc., Middleton, Wisconsin
© 2004 by A-R Editions, Inc.

All rights reserved. No part of this book may be reproduced or transmitted in any form by any electronic or mechanical means (including photocopying, recording, or information storage and retrieval) without permission in writing from the publisher.

The purchase of this edition does not convey the right to perform it in public, nor to make a recording of it for any purpose. Such permission must be obtained in advance from the publisher.

A-R Editions is pleased to support scholars and performers in their use of *Recent Researches* material for study or performance. Subscribers to any of the *Recent Researches* series, as well as patrons of subscribing institutions, are invited to apply for information about our "Copyright Sharing Policy."

Printed in the United States of America

ISBN 0-89579-546-9
ISSN 0193-5364

∞ The paper used in this publication meets the minimum requirements of the American National Standard for Information Sciences—Permanence of Paper for Printed Library Materials, ANSI Z39.48-1984.

Contents

Acknowledgments vi

Introduction vii
  Early History of the Woodwind Quintet vii
  Franz Lachner viii
  Lachner's Quintets x
  Notes xii

Plates xiv

Woodwind Quintet No. 1 in F Major
  [I] Andante; Allegro assai 1
  [II] Scherzo: Allegro assai 25
  [III] Andante; Allegro; Andante 32
  [IV] Allegro 44

Woodwind Quintet No. 2 in E-flat Major
  [I] Allegro 63
  [II] Andante con moto 88
  [III] Menuetto: Allegro assai 106
  [IV] Allegretto 116

Critical Report 139
  Sources 139
  Editorial Method 139
  Critical Notes 143

Acknowledgments

I would like to express my deep appreciation to Wheaton College for granting me a sabbatical and additional funding which led to the start of this project. I am also grateful to the Bayerische Staatsbibliothek for their kind permission to publish these works, and for allowing facsimile plates to be included in the present edition. My thanks also to Murray Lefkowitz and Joel Sheveloff for their ideas, suggestions, and wise council. I am grateful to A-R Editions for their interest in the project, and feel especially indebted to the editorial staff, for their superb guidance and careful attention to detail throughout—I take full responsibility for any remaining errors. Finally, most of all, I must thank my dear wife Susan, and our beautiful daughters, Susannah and Caroline, for their endless patience and unwavering support throughout the entire journey.

Introduction

Early History of the Woodwind Quintet

The woodwind quintet emerged as a genre in the period 1800–1820 with works by Cambini, Danzi, and Reicha, only to lie mostly dormant throughout the remaining years of the nineteenth century. Renewed interest in the genre developed in the 1920s, particularly with Hindemith's *Kleine Kammermusik*, Op. 24/2 (1922), which led to a vast number of wind quintets being composed throughout the twentieth century. Ironically, while the genre remains a vibrant and fertile area for composition in the twenty-first century, scholarship has not kept pace, and there has yet to appear a major monograph in English on the subject.[1]

There are many potential reasons why the wind quintet was not formed until well after the emergence of the string quartet (which arose in the mid eighteenth century). While it would seem logical to feature a chamber group consisting of a representative from each woodwind family, the clarinet was not even regularly included in symphony orchestras until the late eighteenth century.[2] What did exist in the late eighteenth century, had an extensive repertoire, and is generally viewed as the immediate forerunner to the woodwind quintet, however, was the *harmonie*. The *harmonie* was a wind chamber ensemble (one instrument per part) typically consisting of paired oboes, clarinets, bassoons, and horns.[3] While music for a small wind ensemble can be traced to France and even England, the genre reached its greatest flourishing with the founding of a court *harmonie* by Emperor Joseph in 1782; this established a tradition in Vienna (mirrored by several other aristocrats including the Esterhazy family), which solidified the association of the *harmonie* with Austro/Germanic regions. *Harmoniemusik* began to disappear by the early nineteenth century, as the patronage system which sustained it started to crumble. What emerged from this tradition was the woodwind quintet, a grouping of now single wind instruments, providing remarkable variety of color and a wide range of expressive possibilities.[4]

Three composers in particular took advantage of this new combination and found it amenable to their artistic vision; they are crucial to the early history of the woodwind quintet: Giuseppe Cambini, Franz Danzi, and Anton Reicha. With the *harmoniemusik* and the Mozart and Beethoven piano quintets providing wonderful examples of wind chamber music,[5] a group of three woodwind quintets—what seems to be the first of their kind—appeared in Paris, published by Sieber (ca. 1802): *Trois Quintetti Concertans pour Clarinette, Flute, Hautbois, Cor, et Basson*. They were composed by the Italian Giuseppe Maria Cambini (1746–1825).[6] Cambini dedicated the quintets to Jean Xavier Lefebvre, principal clarinettist of the Chapel Royal, who taught at the Paris Conservatoire from its founding (1795) until 1824, and who also wrote an important clarinet *Method* (1802).[7] Cambini's three quintets remain active in the repertoire and display the solid craftsmanship he would have acquired through possible studies with the venerable Padre Martini, Manfredi, or Gossec, the latter being a critical figure in the French musical scene of the time. The writing of the Cambini quintets is witty and quite brilliant, often even reminiscent of the virtuosic woodwind writing of Rossini. The works are all in three movements (fast-slow-fast). Cambini was a prolific composer with some four hundred compositions to his name (including numerous string quartets); and while he was most famous for his operas during his lifetime, he remains best known today for his pioneering work with the woodwind quintet.

Franz Danzi (1763–1826) was part of a large German family of musicians. As a cellist, Danzi entered the famed Mannheim orchestra at the young age of fifteen, and eventually replaced his father as principal cellist of that orchestra in 1784. Danzi spent the years from 1812 until his death as kapellmeister in Karlsruhe, where he turned his attention to chamber music, finding an ally in the publisher Johann Andre. Danzi composed numerous woodwind chamber works, among which are his famous nine woodwind quintets: Op. 56, Nos. 1, 2, 3 (1819–20); Op. 67, Nos. 1, 2, 3 and Op. 68, Nos. 1, 2, 3 (both sets dating from the period 1823–24). Danzi's quintets are recognized as standard literature today. While aspects of his writing might be viewed as pre-romantic (particularly harmonic elements), his style is ultimately conservative and firmly in the mature classical-era tradition. The phrasing is typically periodic and form is strictly followed (e.g., recapitulations tend to be literal in the opening sonata-form movements). All nine works follow the expected four-movement format: sonata form, slow movement, minuet, and rondo (or some other fast-movement ending).

Anton Reicha (1770–1836) remains the most significant pioneer of the woodwind quintet. Czech by birth, he eventually settled in Paris, where in 1818 he was named professor of counterpoint and fugue at the Paris Conservatoire. His treatise on composition (ca. 1818) became the official harmony textbook at the school; it encouraged a practical and progressive approach toward composing which was reflected by Reicha himself in his own works. He was well known, counting Rossini, Mendelssohn, and Ignaz Moscheles among his friends, while his influence as a teacher was also considerable, with Berlioz, Liszt, and Franck listed as his students. Reicha's importance to the woodwind quintet has long been recognized, although often just duly noted.[8] Reicha published twenty-four wind quintets in four sets of six: Op. 88 (1817), Op. 91 (1819), Op. 99 (1819), and Op. 100 (1820); all were published in Paris.[9] Reicha himself realized the importance of these works and emphasized their pioneering nature:

> Let us consider for a minute the twenty-four quintets for wind instruments, truly novel in style which created such a sensation throughout Europe and brought me much renown. At the time there was a dearth not only of good classic music but of any good music for wind instruments, simply because the composers knew little of their technique. The effects which a combination of these instruments could produce had not been explored. . . . Such was the state of affairs when I conceived the idea of writing a quintet for a combination of the five principal wind instruments (flute, oboe, clarinet, horn, and bassoon). My first attempt was a failure, and I discarded it. A new style of composition was necessary for these instruments. They hold the mean between voices and strings. Combinations of a particular kind had to be devised in order to strike the listener. After much thought and careful study of the possibilities of each instrument, I made my second attempt and wrote two very successful quintets. A few years later I had completed the six which make up the first book. I owe their success to those admirable musicians Messieurs Guilou, Vogt, Boufil, Dauprat and Henry whose perfect rendition of them at public concerts and private musicales started all Paris talking about them. Encouraged by their success, I wrote eighteen more, bringing the number to twenty-four. They are published in four books. If the many congratulatory letters I received can be believed, they created a sensation throughout Europe.[10]

Curiously, Reicha makes no mention of Cambini's three quintets which predated his by some fifteen years. It seems highly unlikely that a composer of Reicha's stature would have been unaware of these works which were also published in Paris. Reicha's quintets are highly polished works featuring considerable virtuosity on the part of all instruments (true melody-sharing throughout) and great contrapuntal dexterity; Op. 88, No. 1 features an extended fugue in the last movement. Other notable movements are the first of Op. 88, No. 5, which contains an interesting miniature cadenza for the horn, and the first of Op. 88, No. 2, which opens the exposition proper with an extended bassoon solo.[11] All of his quintets are in four movements, with the first movement typically in sonata form. Reicha was quite lucid and perceptive in viewing his work as a theorist along with these wind quintets as his most important achievements. He ends his memoirs with the following:

> More than a hundred [works] have been published, about sixty are still in manuscript. Among the last will be found my finest efforts, excepting my treatises on composition and the twenty-four quintets for wind instruments.[12]

Reicha's quintets are indeed a significant contribution to the genre and constitute the last great outpouring of wind quintets until the twentieth century.[13]

After Reicha, the woodwind quintet suffered severe neglect, and from the relatively small output of quintets composed throughout the nineteenth century, only three are performed with any regularity: the quintets by August Klughardt, Paul Taffanel, and Charles Lefebvre.[14] No doubt the popularity of the latter two works is due in large measure to their inclusion in Andraud's famous *Twenty-Two Woodwind Quintets,* an anthology used frequently by modern performers.[15] Lefebvre's Suite, Op. 57 is a relatively short, bucolic work in three movements (Canon, Allegro scherzando, and Finale). Both the Taffanel and Klughardt quintets are substantial compositions, although they reflect national propensities: the three-movement French work is a bit lighter and less earnest than its heavier German counterpart, which owes a lot to the influence of Wagner.

It is within this interesting context that we find Lachner's contributions. With both the Taffanel and Klughardt coming well into the nineteenth century, and particularly the latter permeated with fully mature romantic style traits, Lachner's two quintets constitute a significant and crucial link between the early classical vocabulary of Cambini and Danzi and these later works. Thus, Cambini can be viewed as pioneering the woodwind quintet concept, Danzi and particularly Reicha as establishing the genre by 1820, with Lachner contributing important examples in the 1820s, after which the wind quintet was sadly neglected, except for the few works mentioned above. The view of Reicha as the premiere quintet composer of the early nineteenth century due to the quality and quantity of his works remains unchallenged, but the significance of Lachner's contributions to the genre should be clearly acknowledged, and the historical importance of his two quintets fully recognized, especially given the paucity of wind quintets during this period.

Franz Lachner

Franz Lachner (1803–90) was born on 2 April 1803 in the town of Rain am Lech, Germany, where his father, Anton, was the parish organist. Franz was part of a large, musical family and was given piano and organ lessons early on by his father. After the latter's death in 1822, Lachner moved to Munich briefly, before becoming an organist at the Lutheran church in Vienna, an appointment he secured in 1824. During his time in Vienna, he became friends with Schubert[16] and met Beethoven. While keeping his post as organist, Lachner went on to become assistant (1827) and finally chief conductor (1829) of the Kärntnertortheater, one of the two imperial venues in the city. Not much is known of his tenure in Vienna, though his attempt in 1833 to start a professional orchestral concert series using opera house players seems to have failed.[17] In 1834 Lachner went to Mannheim, where he served for two years as kapellmeister. By 1836, Lachner had returned to Munich, where he quickly established himself as one of the leading musicians of that city. He served as chief conductor of the Court Opera (Hofoper) and conducted concerts by the Musikalische Akademie and Königliche Vokalkapelle. When named Generalmusikdirektor in 1852, he became, essentially, the general music director for all of Bavaria. His reputation and the high esteem of his leadership seem well established at this point.[18] While his skills as a composer were perhaps overshadowed by his conducting, they were nevertheless certainly recognized; the French scholar François-Joseph Fétis, writing in the mid nineteenth century, says:

> Lachner is justly considered in Germany as one of the most remarkable artists of the present time, not only as a composer, but also as a music conductor. His is a serious talent, solid, belonging to one of the better traditions of the old school [ancienne école], which unfortunately is being erased day by day in his country.[19]

Likewise, the German encyclopedist Gustav Schilling ranks him high amongst contemporary musicians.[20] There seems little doubt, then, that Lachner served as the leading musician in Munich during the thirty-year period 1836–66, and was instrumental in establishing Munich's reputation as a major operatic center.

By the 1860s, however, this rich and fruitful period for Lachner came to a rather sudden halt with the rising popularity of Richard Wagner. Throughout Lachner's tenure, the Munich Hofoper had mounted productions of works by Beethoven, Mozart, and the contemporary composers Spohr, Marschner, and Flotow. With a performance of *Ernani* in 1848, Lachner even started a series of performances of Verdi's operas (Verdi himself conducted several of the German premieres of his works in Munich). Lachner's ties to Wagner, however, were much more tenuous. While conducting the Munich premieres of *Tannhäuser* (1855) and *Lohengrin* (1858), Lachner did not fully embrace Wagner's musical style and, more to the point, became increasingly uncomfortable with the close bonds (especially after 1864) between Wagner and the new eighteen-year-old King Ludwig II of Bavaria; these growing ties clearly proclaimed Wagner as the rising star. This was confirmed in October 1864, when King Ludwig made available to Wagner the spacious and extravagantly decorated house at 21 Briennerstrasse in Munich. In 1865, Lachner finally applied for his retirement. The growing influence of Wagner on Ludwig, however, was creating tension amongst court circles and the populace at large. The ideas of a Wagnerian theater and a national school of music, both promoted by Wagner, were rejected by an increasingly concerned Munich public. Even Ludwig was forced to recognize the resultant erosion of popular support caused by his uncritical allegiance to Wagner, a recognition which finally led him to request Wagner's departure from Munich in December 1865.

While there had been some confrontations between Wagner and Lachner, the latter graciously suggested Wagner be awarded the Royal Maximilian Order in 1873. After having been retired for some fifteen years, Lachner himself was not forgotten by a grateful Munich, which named him honorary citizen in 1883 (ironically, the year Wagner died). During these retirement years, Lachner typically spent the summers at Bernried, on Lake Starnberg, where the young composer Englebert Humperdinck studied privately with him during the summer of 1877; Humperdinck provides a moving portrait of the revered aging maestro through his many letters.[21] Franz Lachner died in Munich on 20 January 1890.

While clearly best known as a conductor, Lachner was also a prolific composer, having written four operas, eight symphonies (1828–51), seven orchestral suites, eight masses, over two hundred songs, numerous keyboard works, and a considerable amount of chamber music. The latter includes a septet (1824) and nonet (1875) for mixed strings and winds; six string quartets (1843–75); two piano quartets (1868–69); two piano trios (1828, 1830); a trio for clarinet, horn, and piano (1830); the octet for winds (1850); and the two woodwind quintets (1824, 1827).[22]

Both Lachner's quintets date from an early period in his life. Quintet No. 1 in F Major, dating 1824, was written when the composer was just twenty-one, a year after he received his appointment as organist of the Protestant Church in Vienna. The Quintet No. 2 in E-flat Major was written just three years later, in 1827, the year he was appointed assistant chief conductor of the Kärntnertortheater. The two quintets can thus be seen as works of youth, which coincide with important moments in Lachner's life. Given this chronology, one especially striking aspect of Lachner's quintets is the idiomatic nature of their lines. The writing for winds is expertly crafted, almost as if the composer were writing for the woodwind section of an orchestra; there is, at times, an orchestral element in chamber guise. Another important point to keep in mind was Lachner's exposure to the rich tradition of Vienna throughout the 1820s, especially to the works of Beethoven and Schubert. We know that Lachner and Schubert became close friends (Schubert was, after all, just six years older than Lachner), and the influence of Schubert on Lachner is unmistakable. Like Schubert, Lachner's artistic vision was clearly shaped by Viennese classicism, but also like Schubert, he saw beyond this, and incorporated rhapsodic and progressive elements into his music. It is precisely this rhapsodic trait within the genre of the woodwind quintet that makes Lachner's work so fascinating and historically significant. While we find elements of classicism in his music, we also find lyrical flights of fancy and interesting harmonic twists which look ahead; although Lachner never achieved Schubert's lyrical and harmonic genius, the ties can be heard. It is interesting to find both composers writing chamber works for mixed ensemble in the same year of 1824, Schubert's octet and Lachner's septet; perhaps these two works in turn looked to Beethoven's enormously popular septet (1800) for inspiration.[23]

Given this rich history for the wind quintet during the period 1800–1820, it is truly surprising to find so little written for it after Lachner. Lachner himself composed his octet (for winds, 1850) and nonet (combining a string quartet and wind quintet, 1875), but never returned to the woodwind quintet, leaving just these two remarkable and youthful works as his sole venture into the genre.[24]

Lachner's Quintets

The autograph manuscripts for both Lachner quintets are in the Bayerische Staatsbibliothek, Munich; these were the only sources used for the present edition.[25]

Quintet No. 1 in F Major was composed in 1824 and consists of four movements. The third-movement complex is quite interesting and almost could deceive one into viewing it as two separate movements. Indeed, the Andante which starts the third movement ends with a Dal segno il [rather than "al"] Fine indication, which would seem to unequivocally denote the conclusion of one movement and the start of another. The following Allegro, however, has no meter given in the score (as would be expected with a new movement), starts with an upbeat which "completes" the previous "Fine" measure, and, most significantly, appears to be based on the measure 29 motive from the Andante section. Thus, what emerges is a type of variation-form complex (see below for a detailed discussion of this movement).[26]

The first movement is a large sonata-form structure in F major, which constitutes the longest (422 measures) movement in either of Lachner's quintets. It consists of an introductory Andante (mm. 1–26), which is proleptic in that it presents, in lyrical fashion, the contour of what sets forth, beginning at measure 27 (and now in 3/4 meter), as the first theme of the main Allegro assai. Throughout the opening, periodicity is clearly evident, as is the repetition of phrases an octave higher (e.g., mm. 1–8 repeated at mm. 9–16) in order to achieve variety of tone color. An effective repartee section begins at measure 43 involving all instruments and even featuring stretto textures (mm. 57–58, 63–64). An interesting pairing of voices occurs in the passage beginning measure 69 where the flute and clarinet are paired off against the oboe and bassoon, but then the oboe and clarinet are paired off against the flute and bassoon. A second theme (in a fully established dominant C major) is arrived at in measure 135. While in a new key, and heard as a distinct and fresh theme, the motive shares much in terms of melodic and rhythmic contouring with the first theme and is less lyrical than the theme heard at measure 105. The tail of this secondary theme involves an effective contrary-motion passage for flute and bassoon (m. 139 and following). An interesting closing section (beginning at m. 167) features an inverted pedal (in the flute) over the melody below. The development opens in severe counterpoint (m. 205), simulating although not actually creating a strict canon. After a nice repartee section between oboe and clarinet (beginning at m. 224), a powerful dominant pedal in the horn and bassoon (m. 240) announces the gradual move toward the recapitulation. The latter begins at measure 262 and brings in the stretto-like texture almost immediately (mm. 278–85), climaxing on the diminished seventh chord at measure 289. Lachner uses dynamics for dramatic purposes here, with *f* and *pp* markings in close proximity. The second theme returns (in the tonic) at measure 347, with the inverted-pedal closing section coming back at measure 379. A coda, marked "Più mosso" (m. 404), rounds off the movement.

The second movement is a scherzo, consisting of rather straightforward music placed in a somewhat uncommon position.[27] The movement is in the relative minor (D minor) and uses a 9/8 meter, subdivided in three beats throughout. Lachner often pairs the flute and oboe (they play in octaves from the opening to m. 10, and mm. 23–51), and the clarinet and horn, with the bassoon providing the rhythmic propulsion on the downbeat. The trio changes key to the parallel major (D major), and comes to a ♩♪ rhythm (instead of the running eighths heard earlier), but keeps the flute/oboe doubling, and on the whole comes across as rather static. The structure is typical: both scherzo and trio sections are in two parts, with the former played da capo after the trio concludes.

The third movement is rather elaborate and starts with an Andante in F major which shifts the meter to 2/4. The movement as a whole opens with an intriguing ternary (A :||: A' :||: B :||: B' || A" A''' A") structure (see mm. 1–80), with the B section in the parallel F minor. The theme heard at the beginning is lyrical and flowing, and it is embellished considerably in its return (m. 53) after the B couplet. This middle B section contrasts a march-like motive (m. 29) with a flowing theme passed gently amongst the horn, flute, and clarinet (mm. 37–44). At measure 72 in the source we find noted "Dal # il Fine," and while there is no "Fine" marked in the autograph manuscript, Lachner makes his intentions clear by placing the segno above measure 53 (using # rather than the modern sign), numbering measures 53–72 as bars 1–20, and adding a second ending numbered as bar 28, given the repetition of bars 1–7 as bars 21–27 (see plate 4). Thus, the fermatas in the source's second ending confirm that this is the "Fine" bar, which is followed by a double barline.[28] After the brief fermata, functioning as a clarifying aesthetic pause, Lachner begins a subtle Allegro variation on the B section's F-minor motive which sounds severely contrapuntal (almost canonic) and divides into two repeated sections. This lasts all of twenty-four measures before the final section, labeled "Andante," appears and appropriately shifts back to F major and provides the most virtuosic variation of the movement (sextuplet sixteenths), this time varying the material from the opening itself. The structure of the movement from measure 81, therefore, is Bvar :||: B'var :||: Avar :||: A'var Coda.

The final movement is an Allegro in cut time. The sonata-form structure is fairly straightforward, with texture and pairings emerging as the most interesting elements of the movement. The opening theme starts in the flute's low range but then moves to wide leaps for all instruments which lead toward the typical parallel runs heard often in Lachner (this time featuring flute, oboe, and clarinet). Other pairings follow (flute/clarinet at mm. 25–26 and oboe/horn at mm. 27 and 29). A bridge section provides constantly shifting textures, for even further pairings which produce a beautiful variety of tone colors (mm. 33–60). The second theme (in C major) enters at measure 61 in the flute, doubled an octave lower by the oboe. What appears as a closing section emerges at measure 79, this time pairing the flute and oboe in thirds, and with an odd answering phrase which rises rather than descends at its end (compare mm. 79–81 with mm. 83–85). A rather short development section ensues, punctuated by dynamic contrasts (mm. 95–98), some of which are rather abrupt (mm. 103–5). An effective return is initiated by cumulative entries (starting at m. 120) over a dominant pedal in the horn (and later bassoon); these blossom into parallel runs by the flute, oboe, and clarinet, which lead to the recapitulation at measure 128. The recapitulation is in textbook fashion with secondary material in the tonic (F major). The movement concludes with a coda marked "Più mosso" (m. 247). This climactic finish again features interesting pairings (mostly flute/oboe versus clarinet/horn), and ends with a marvelously effective inverted tonic chord (pedal) in the flute, oboe, and clarinet, over a gradually ascending, then descending bass-line arpeggio in the horn and bassoon.

Quintet No. 2 in E-flat Major dates from 1827 and consists of four movements: Allegro, Andante con moto, Menuetto, and Allegretto. It is interesting that Lachner abandoned the more progressive scheme of his first quintet—with its second-movement scherzo and its complex-structured third movement—returning instead to the traditional ordering of movements, including a third-movement minuet. In spite of these seemingly conservative alterations, however, this second quintet is considerably more confident and the more mature of the two works. Thus, the "traditional" approach notwithstanding, this second quintet is bold and remarkable in several ways, particularly with its interesting modulations and idiomatic, colorful use of instruments. The first movement is in sonata form and opens with a powerful unison "Ur-motive" in all voices, which, once stated, surprisingly gets immediately repeated a step lower (see plate 6). The point of imitation which follows uses the same octave motive and is beautifully passed between flute, bassoon, and oboe. The first theme proper (which fleshes out the octave motive) is introduced with a beautiful doubling (oboe/clarinet) at measure 12. An effective repartee between flute and clarinet occurs beginning in measure 20. One interesting trait of the octave "Ur-motive" is its ability to modulate in numerous directions. These unexpected harmonic movements are exemplified beginning at measure 31, where the motive moves chromatically, abruptly, and somewhat ambiguously toward B-flat minor (m. 37)! There follows some bridge and extension material which finally introduces the second theme in the dominant (B-flat major) at measure 56. Dialogue between flute and oboe climaxes at measure 70 with a striking effect achieved by parallel runs in the flute, oboe, and clarinet; this is counterbalanced by a virtuosic contrary-motion passage in the bassoon (mm. 71–72). The closing section of the exposition begins at measure 76 with playful, virtuosic figurations in the clarinet accompanying the horn solo; this is repeated at measure 90 with the flute replacing the horn as soloist. The development is typically heralded by an abrupt modulation followed by stasis, as if Lachner were considering his options (mm. 104–7). The actual move into the development (m. 107) is extremely effective, using the clarinet run reminiscent of the second theme's lead-in. The development opens, interestingly, with a variant of the first theme, now in D-flat major. The passage at measure 116 features a beautiful texture via paired horn and bassoon in parallel motion across the range with the flute. There follows various intriguing and surprising modulations, all using the potentially ambiguous octave "Ur-motive" (e.g., m. 146ff.). This leads deftly to the recapitulation (beginning at m. 163), heralding a return of the first theme in the tonic, E-flat major (m. 170). The minor excursion (now relative minor) is visited (m. 199), followed by one of the most exquisite moments in the movement: the gentle and ingenious connecting passage (especially mm. 207–17) to the second theme variant (m. 229), now in the tonic. The virtuosic closing is mirrored from the exposition with the flute now given the demanding figurations. The coda (beginning at m. 261) wraps up the movement brilliantly, with a few nice harmonic surprises and effective repartee between the oboe and horn.

The second movement is a beautifully lilting Andante con moto in $\frac{3}{4}$ meter set in the subdominant key of A-flat major. It opens with a periodic 4 + 4 sequential statement, answered by a deftly configured 2 + 2 + 4 phrase. Instead of cadencing on the last beat of measure 16, however (as was his custom up to this point), Lachner cadences on the first half of beat two, and uses the last three eighths as an anacrusis to the following phrase—a line featuring a wonderful pairing of the flute and bassoon in parallel motion. The indecision which one senses starting at measure 29 reaches its apotheosis in the marvelously odd static pedal of the horn at measures 37–40. A new theme emerges at measure 63, which begins its full blossoming at measure 76, when Lachner writes a truly beautiful repartee of this theme between the clarinet, oboe, and flute. This leads, in turn, to yet another lyrical theme at measure 93 (in the dominant, E-flat major), played by the oboe. The lyricism of this line and the idiomatic writing throughout highlight this section. Some intriguing harmonic modulations are heard beginning at measure 113, with a moving and gentle return to the first theme in the tonic (A-flat major) at measure 152. The other main themes follow, now also in the tonic, with slight changes of instrument designation (e.g., the clarinet/horn pairing which began at m. 93 is now changed to oboe/clarinet, starting at m. 191). After a final flurry of triplets and sextuplets, the horn begins a reflective closing section, using, appropriately enough, the material of measure 76, now as then, beautifully touched on by all.

The third movement, while marked "Menuetto," certainly has all the playfulness and energy of a scherzo. It is in the tonic (E-flat major) and features the typical minuet-trio-minuet format. The main theme is a tutti unison drop of a diminished fourth which resolves up a half step. The drop itself is into a trilled dotted half note which gives the passage great momentum and bounce. Moreover, the phrasing sets up four measures of leaps, counterbalanced nicely with four measures of scalar motion. The variant beginning after the first repeat bar (m. 17) cleverly elaborates this second answering phrase (oboe, mm. 20–23). This same section also displays Lachner's ingenious "hocketing" effect between flute and oboe, which takes advantage of their similar, yet unique colors (mm. 18, 20, 24, 26). The end of the minuet section is emphasized by a trill for bassoon on a low B-flat(!)—rather unusual. The trio section does not really reduce the texture or change the key (E-flat). Like the previous minuet section, the trio is in two parts, with the second featuring several dramatic thirty-second-note runs in octaves (mm. 121, 125). Throughout the movement (as indeed is true of the entire quintet), the orchestral, idiomatic nature of Lachner's writing for wind instruments is evident. It truly sounds like the woodwind section of an orchestra playing chamber music, not unlike a concertante section of an orchestral work.

Lachner concludes the quintet with a sprightly Allegretto set in $^6_8$ meter. This last movement is in clear sonata form with E-flat as the tonic. While the opening theme itself is rather prosaic melodically, Lachner maintains rhythmic interest by starting on the second eighth note (though it could sound like a downbeat), with the use of an accent on the third eighth note of measure 2, creating a type of hemiola in measures 2–3. Bridge material, commencing at measure 19, features a flamboyant thirty-second-note ascending-octave run passed between the flute, oboe, and clarinet. At measure 41 the bassoon joins in the octave runs leading to a secondary dominant pedal, which ultimately ushers in the second theme at measure 48, a beautifully lyrical section marked "con espress[ione]" and set in the dominant, B-flat major. The oboe has the melody, supported subtly by the horn pedal note and the punctuated chords of the flute, clarinet, and bassoon. The phrasing beginning at measure 64 is especially interesting and Lachner's play with cadences is also noteworthy (e.g., the "extended" nature of the phrase beginning in m. 69 makes the placement of the cadence at m. 72 somewhat unpredictable). Notice also how Lachner cadences measure 67 by the fourth eighth-note beat, while at measure 71 he waits until the downbeat of the next measure (m. 72) to resolve. The passage leading to the closing material stresses the second triplet grouping, creating further rhythmic uncertainty and interest (mm. 83, 88, 90). The thirty-second-note octave runs (from m. 95), heard earlier in the bridge section, and now in contrary motion between bassoon, clarinet, and flute, herald the closing of the exposition, powerfully punctuated with tutti eighth-note unisons. The development lasts some fifty-one measures and features effective repartee between all instruments. A wonderful exchange between flute and bassoon across the range begins at measure 141, climaxing with another tutti passage in unison. A subtle vacillating between B-flat and A in the flute line ushers in the recapitulation at measure 163, with a few variants such as the nice clarinet lead (mm. 218–19) into the second theme (now in the tonic and accompanied with a more elaborate bass line). Also interesting are the harmonic modulations beginning at measure 261 and the extended delay before the cadence at measure 278. The movement ends with the attention-grabbing tutti unison passage, a brief repose (m. 308), and the emphatic, final chords.

Notes

1. See Miroslav Hosek, *Das Bläserquintett: The Woodwind Quintet*, trans. Colleen Gruben (Grunwald: B. Bruchle, 1979). Hosek briefly discusses origins and acoustics, then provides an extended listing of quintet literature, performing groups, and a bibliography. See also Udo Sirker, *Die Entwicklung des Bläserquintetts in der ersten Hälfte des 19 Jahrhunderts* (Regensburg: Bosse, 1968), and Adolf Marold, *Spiel in kleinen Gruppen* (Tutzing: Schneider, 1999). Repertoire listings include: Harry B. Peters, *The Literature of the Woodwind Quintet* (Metuchen, N.J.: Scarecrow, 1971); Barbara Secrist-Schmedes, *Wind Chamber Music: Winds with Piano and Woodwind Quintets—An Annotated Guide* (Lanham, Md.: Scarecrow, 1996); and John Baron, *Chamber Music: A Research and Information Guide* (New York: Garland, 1987).

2. Haydn only includes the clarinet in five of his symphonies (nos. 99, 100, 101, 103, 104); even Mozart, who loved the instrument, uses it only in four of his symphonies (nos. 31, 35, 39, 40)—needless to say, he also has some spectacular wind chamber music featuring clarinets, but alas, no woodwind quintets.

3. See *The New Grove Dictionary of Music and Musicians*, 2d ed. (hereafter *NG2*), s.v. "Harmoniemusik," by Roger Hellyer. See also Antonio Rosetti, *Five Wind Partitas: Music for the Oettingen-Wallerstein Court*, ed. Sterling E. Murray, Recent Researches in the Music of the Classical Era, vols. 30–31 (Madison: A-R Editions, 1989). Among the numerous works written for the *harmonie* one finds the beautiful serenades by Mozart (K. 375 and K. 388).

4. What seems inconceivable is that nobody pursued the piano quintet (oboe, clarinet, bassoon, horn, and piano), a combination so brilliantly created by Mozart (K. 452) and copied by Beethoven (Op. 16). With these two superlative works serving as models, that such a combination was not emulated by other composers is truly a perplexing mystery.

5. One should also keep in mind the enormous popularity of Beethoven's septet (clarinet, bassoon, horn, violin, viola, cello, and bass) which came out in 1800; notwithstanding the use of mixed strings and winds, its effectiveness can hardly have gone unnoticed.

6. Mistakenly named Giovanni Giuseppe [Jean-Joseph] by Fétis in his *Biographie universelle* of 1844 (and hence by many editors since then). Mozart thought Cambini responsible for the Concert Spirituel canceling a performance of his Symphonie concertante, K. 297b (see the letter to his father from Paris, dated 1 May 1778). This is ironic, considering the work featured solo woodwinds, precisely the combination (minus flute) Cambini was to pioneer with his new wind quintets.

7. Not to be confused with Charles Edouard Lefebvre (1843–1917), who composed the beautiful Suite, Op. 57 for woodwind quintet, and who also joined the Paris Conservatoire (1895).

8. "Reicha's wind quintets show his refined sense of instrumental colour and have served as models of their genre." See *NG2*, s.v. "Reicha, Antoine" (p. 131), by Peter Eliot Stone.

9. In addition, there are four movements for quintet published in his treatise, *Traité de haute composition musicale* (Paris, 1824–26). Reicha also composed an early wind quintet in F major (Prague: Panton, 1989), dated 1811. See Olga Sotolova, *Antonin Reicha: A Biography and Thematic Catalogue,* trans. Derek Viney (Prague: Supraphone, 1990).

10. J. G. Prod'homme, "From the Unpublished Autobiography of Anton Reicha," *Musical Quarterly* 22 (1936): 349–50.

11. This last work is probably the best known of Reicha's quintets, but unfortunately most modern editions use a version which cuts out around one-third of the original.

12. Prod'homme, "Anton Reicha," 350.

13. See Millard M. Laing, "Anton Reicha's Quintets for Flute, Oboe, Clarinet, Horn, and Bassoon" (thesis, University of Michigan, 1952); Maurice Emmanuel, *Antonin Reicha: Biographie critique* (Paris: Laurens, 1937); Sotolova, *Antonin Reicha*; Noel H. Magee, "Anton Reicha as Theorist" (Ph.D. diss., University of Iowa, 1977); JoRenee McCachren, "Antoine Reicha's Theories of Musical Form" (Ph.D. diss., University of Texas, 1989); Nancy Baker, "An Ars Poetica for Music: Reicha's System of Syntax and Structure," in *Musical Humanism and Its Legacy: Essays in Honor of Claude V. Palisca* (Stuyvesant, N.Y.: Pendragon, 1992), 419–49.

14. The three quintets by Henri Brod are known but infrequently performed. Likewise, the Quintet in F (1852) by Georges Onslow, while known, is rarely performed.

15. *Twenty-Two Woodwind Quintets,* compiled and revised by Albert Andraud (San Antonio, Tex.: Southern, 1958).

16. Lachner and Schubert remained good friends until the latter's death in 1828. We know Lachner organized informal performances of Schubert's music, commonly referred to as "Schubertiades."

17. See *NG2*, s.v. "Vienna, §5: 1806–1945" (pp. 560–61), by Leon Botstein.

18. In addition to the duties mentioned above, Lachner was involved in leading several music festivals throughout Europe: Munich (1855, 1863), Aachen (1861, 1870), and Salzburg (1855). It should also be noted that Lachner counted several important cultural leaders among his friends, including the poet Eduard Möricke (*Mozart nach Prague,* [1856]) and the historian Felix Dahn (*Politik,* [1835]).

19. François-Joseph Fétis, *Biographie universelle des musiciens,* 2d ed., vol. 5 (Paris: Didot, 1867), 154 [my translation].

20. See Gustav Schilling, *Encyclopädie der gesammten musikalischen Wissenschaften, oder Universal-Lexicon der Tonkunst,* Supplement-Band (Stuttgart: Köhler, 1842), 259–61.

21. See Engelbert Humperdinck, *Briefe und Tagebücher,* vol. 1 (1863–80), ed. Hans-Josef Irmen (Köln: Arno, 1975).

22. While *The New Grove* (both editions) and *Die Musik in Geschichte und Gegenwart* list the works as dating from 1823 and 1829, respectively, "Wien 1824" is very clearly written in the bottom right of the title page for the first quintet, and "1827" in pencil is clearly marked on the upper right of the title page for the second quintet (compare plates 1 and 5); without conclusive proof to the contrary, these autograph manuscript dates will be used as authoritative.

23. Both Schubert and Beethoven use clarinet, bassoon, horn, violin, viola, cello, and bass (with Schubert adding a second violin); Lachner substitutes a flute for the bassoon. Also interesting in this context is Schubert's delightful Octet, D. 72 (1813!) for paired winds.

24. See also Anton Würz, *Franz Lachner als dramatischer Komponist* (Munich: Knorr & Hirth, 1927); Günter Wagner, *Franz Lachner als Liederkomponist* (Chiemsee: Katzbichler, 1970); Jürgen Wulf, *Die geistliche Vokalmusik Franz Lachners* (Hildesheim: Olms, 1999).

25. For physical descriptions of the sources, see the critical report. Quintet No. 1 has been edited by Willem Middelhoven (Amsterdam: Edition Compusic, 1992), while Quintet No. 2 was edited by Frans Vester (Monteux: Musica Rara, 1984), but is no longer in print.

26. There is also the question of two versions for the first two movements in the autograph manuscript. This issue is discussed in the critical report.

27. Beethoven wrote a scherzo for the second movement of his Symphony No. 9; Schubert only used a scherzo twice in his symphonies (nos. 6 and 9) and in both instances as a third movement. Danzi and Reicha would typically use a "menuetto" in the third movement slot.

28. In the edition, the repetition of measures 53–59 plus the second-ending measure has been written out as measures 73–80, making it possible to remove the "Dal # il Fine" indication and the segno (see plate 4). The "Fine" bar therefore corresponds to measure 80.

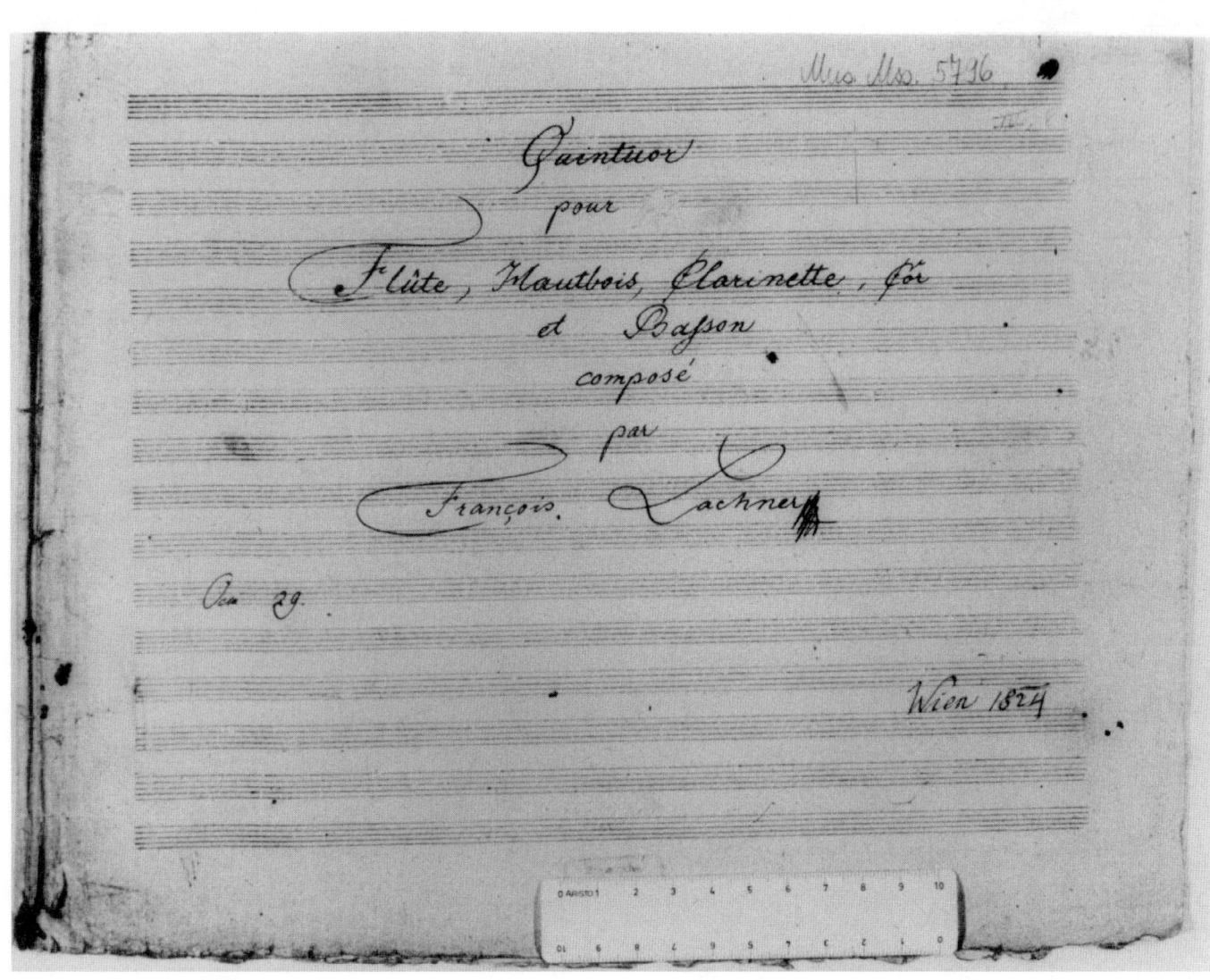

Plate 1. Franz Lachner, Woodwind Quintet No. 1 in F Major (1824), title page. Courtesy of the Bayerische Staatsbibliothek, Munich.

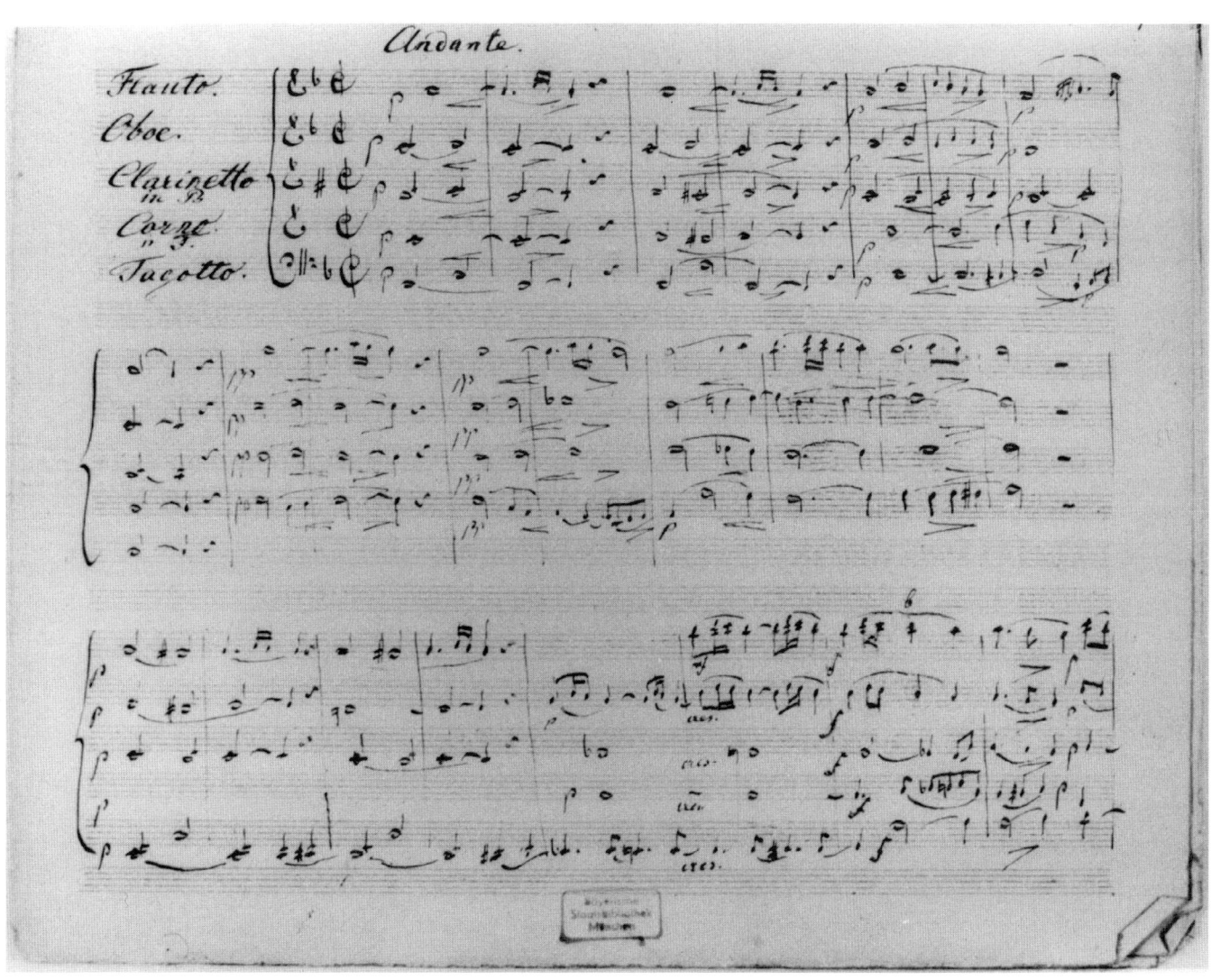

Plate 2. Franz Lachner, Woodwind Quintet No. 1 in F Major (1824), opening of first movement, revised version. Courtesy of the Bayerische Staatsbibliothek, Munich.

Plate 3. Franz Lachner, Woodwind Quintet No. 1 in F Major (1824), opening of first movement, original version. Courtesy of the Bayerische Staatsbibliothek, Munich.

Plate 4. Franz Lachner, Woodwind Quintet No. 1 in F Major (1824), third movement, measures 53–72, with the second ending corresponding to measure 80. Courtesy of the Bayerische Staatsbibliothek, Munich.

Plate 5. Franz Lachner, Woodwind Quintet No. 2 in E-flat Major (1827), title page. Courtesy of the Bayerische Staatsbibliothek, Munich.

Plate 6. Franz Lachner, Woodwind Quintet No. 2 in E-flat Major (1827), opening of first movement. Courtesy of the Bayerische Staatsbibliothek, Munich.

Woodwind Quintet No. 1 in F Major

[I]

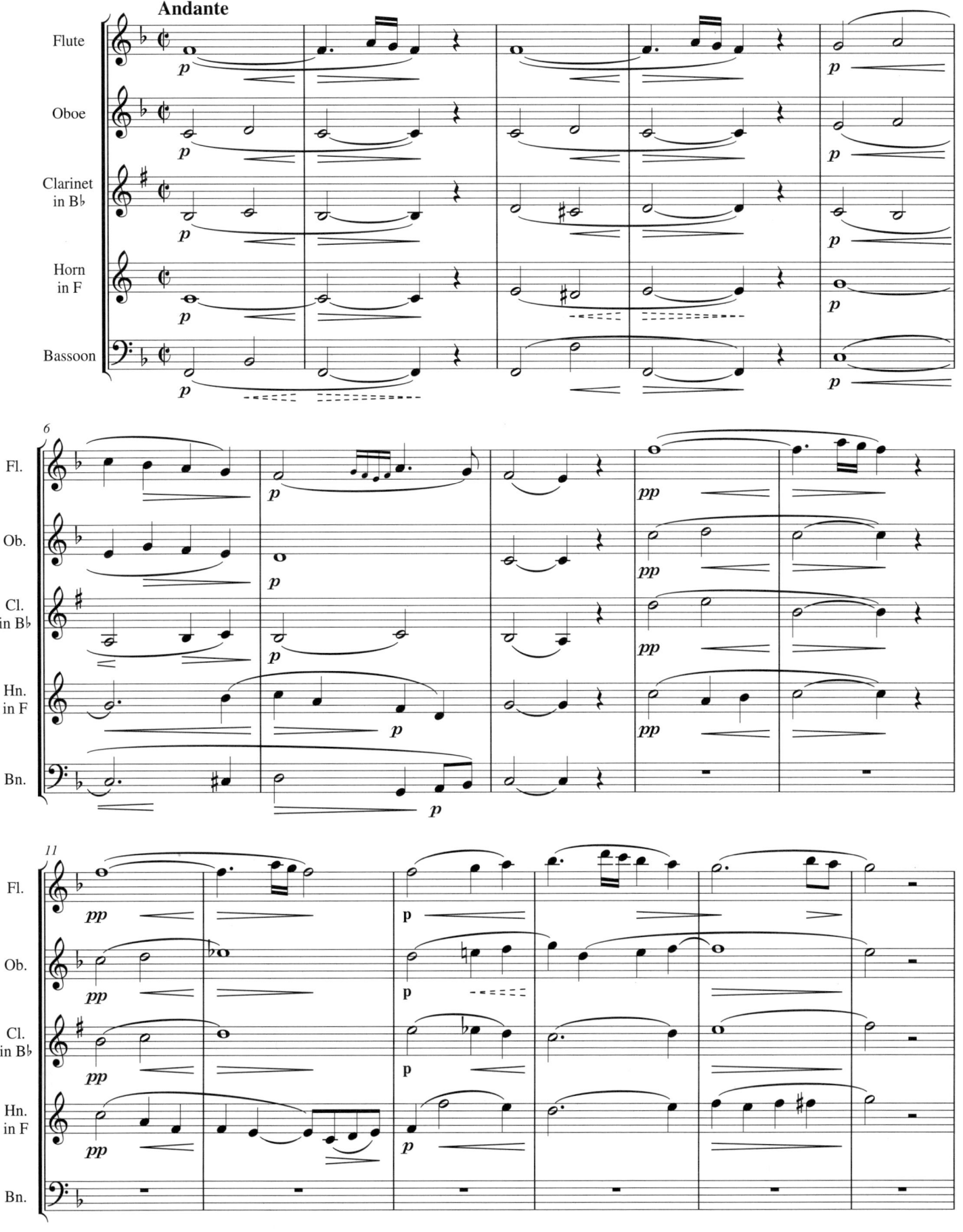

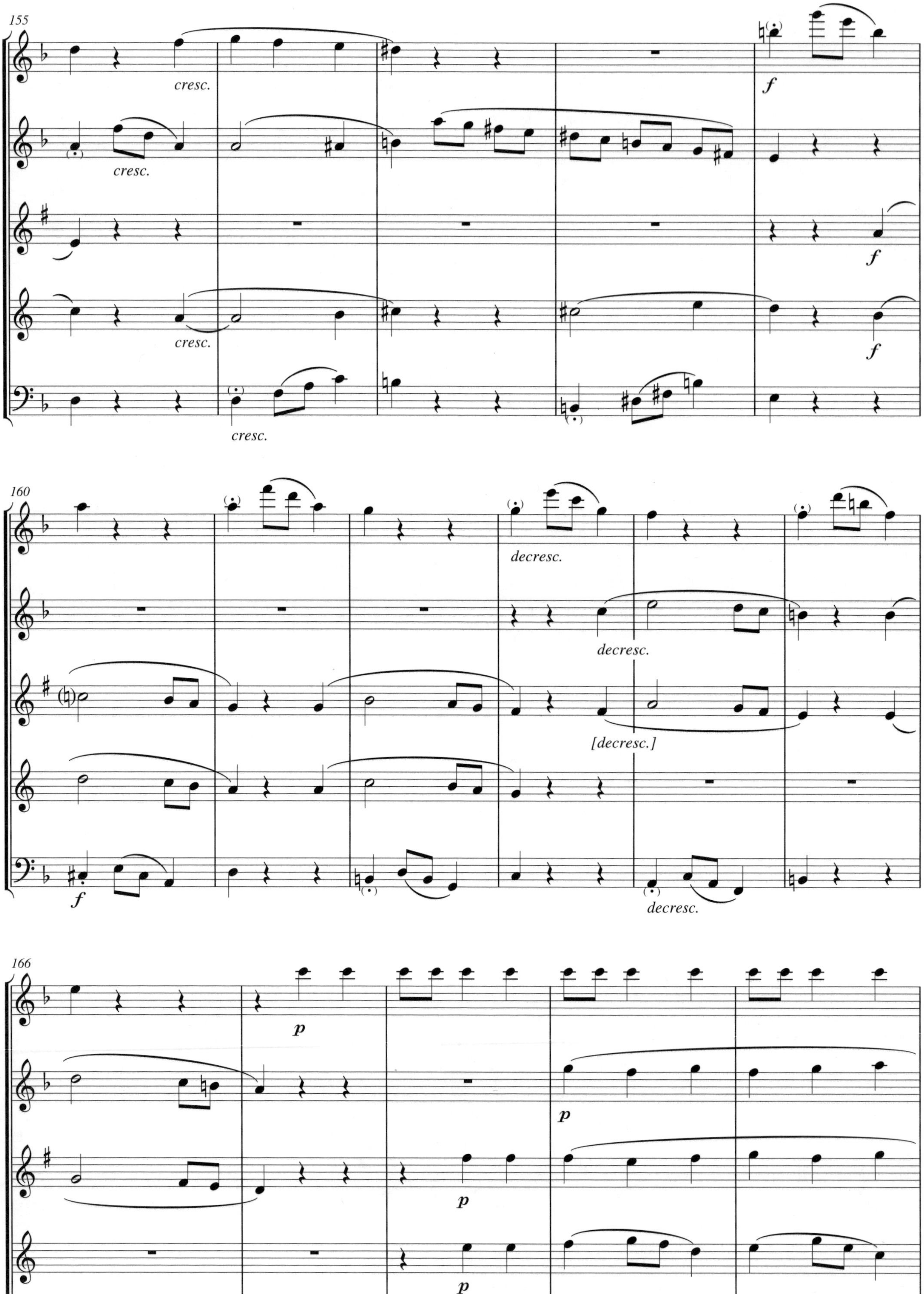
155
Fl.
Ob.
Cl. in B♭
Hn. in F
Bn.
cresc.
cresc.
cresc.
cresc.
f
f
f
160
f
decresc.
decresc.
[decresc.]
decresc.
166
p
p
p
p

14

243
Fl.
Ob.
Cl. in B♭
Hn. in F
Bn.
cresc.
cresc.
cresc.
fp
sfp
sfz
sfz
250
f
sfz
p
257

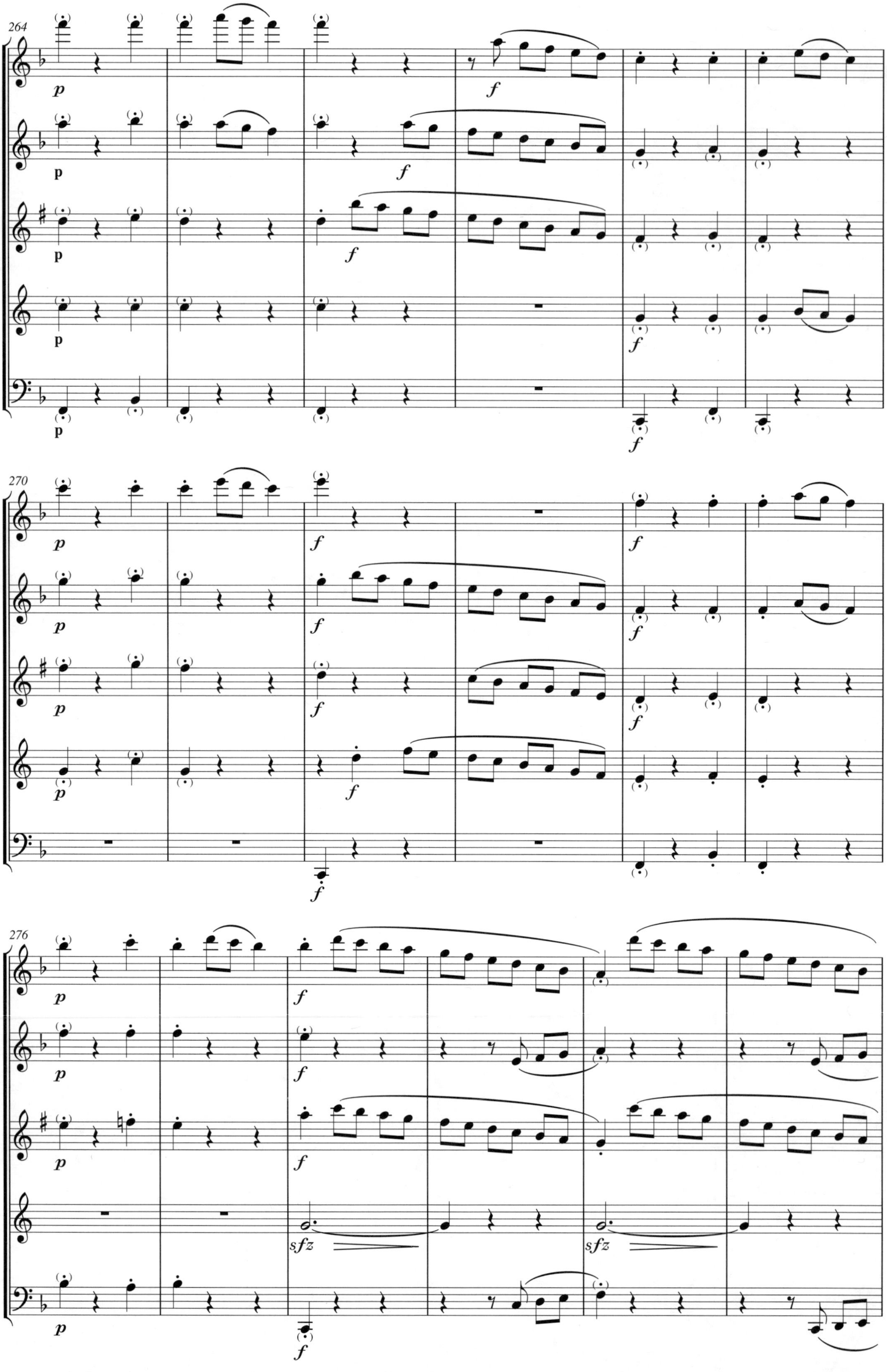
264
Fl.
Ob.
Cl.
in B♭
Hn.
in F
Bn.
p
f
270
276
sfz

17

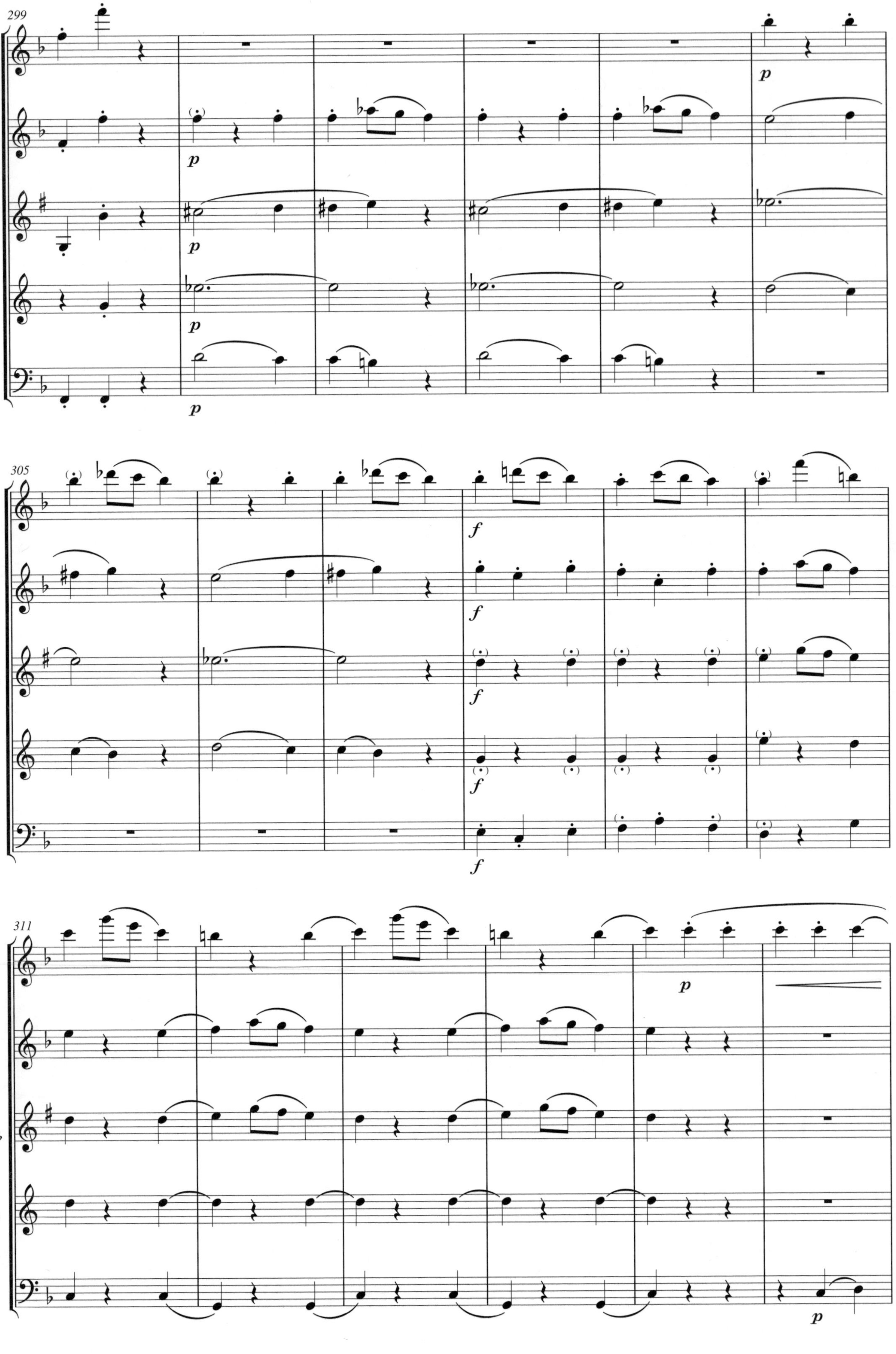
299
Fl.
Ob.
Cl. in B♭
Hn. in F
Bn.
p
305
f
311

19

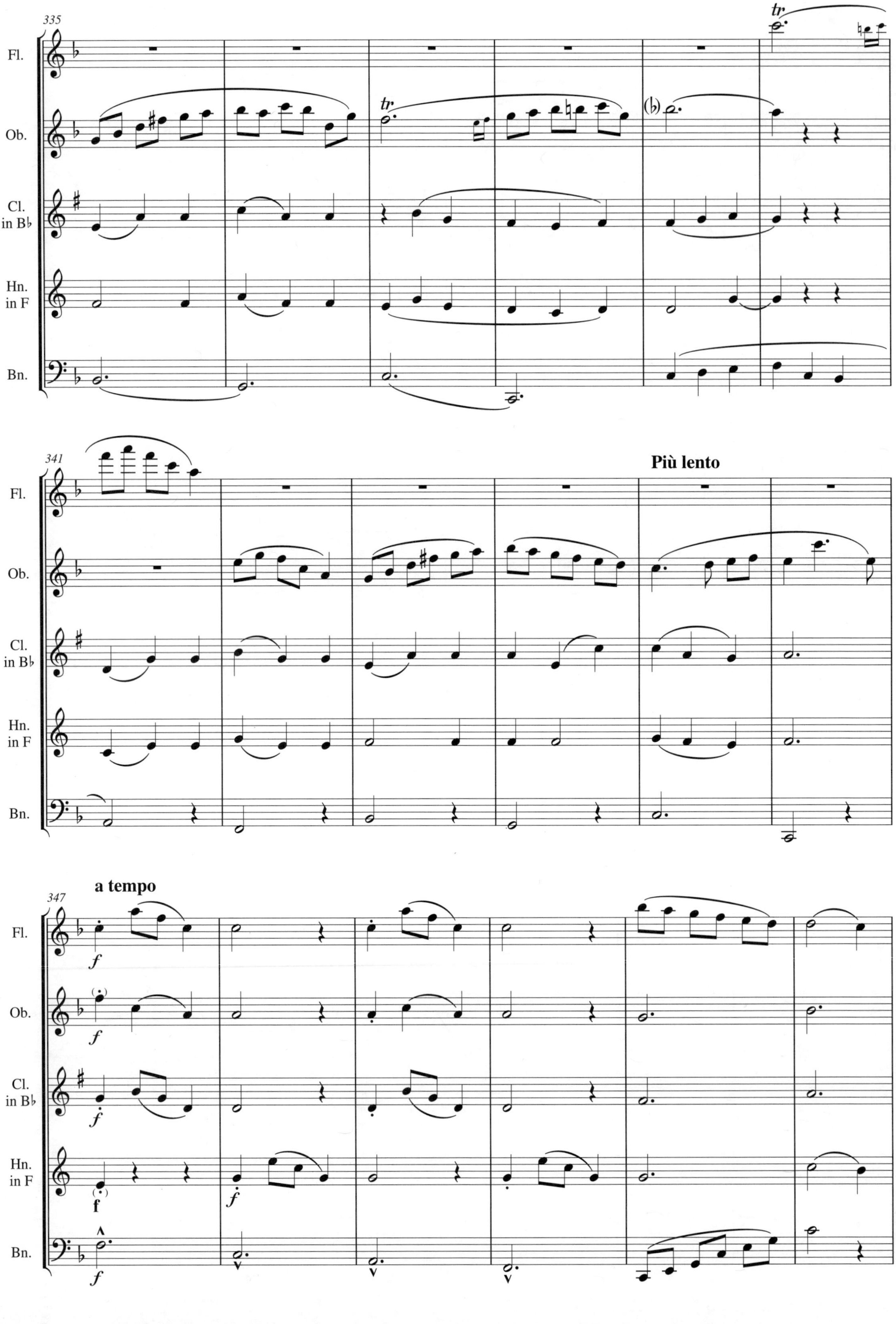
335
Fl.
Ob.
Cl. in B♭
Hn. in F
Bn.
tr
341
Più lento
347
a tempo
f

353
Fl.
Ob.
Cl. in B♭
Hn. in F
Bn.
359
Fl.
Ob.
Cl. in B♭
Hn. in F
Bn.
365
Fl.
Ob.
cresc.
Cl. in B♭
cresc.
Hn. in F
cresc.
Bn.
cresc.

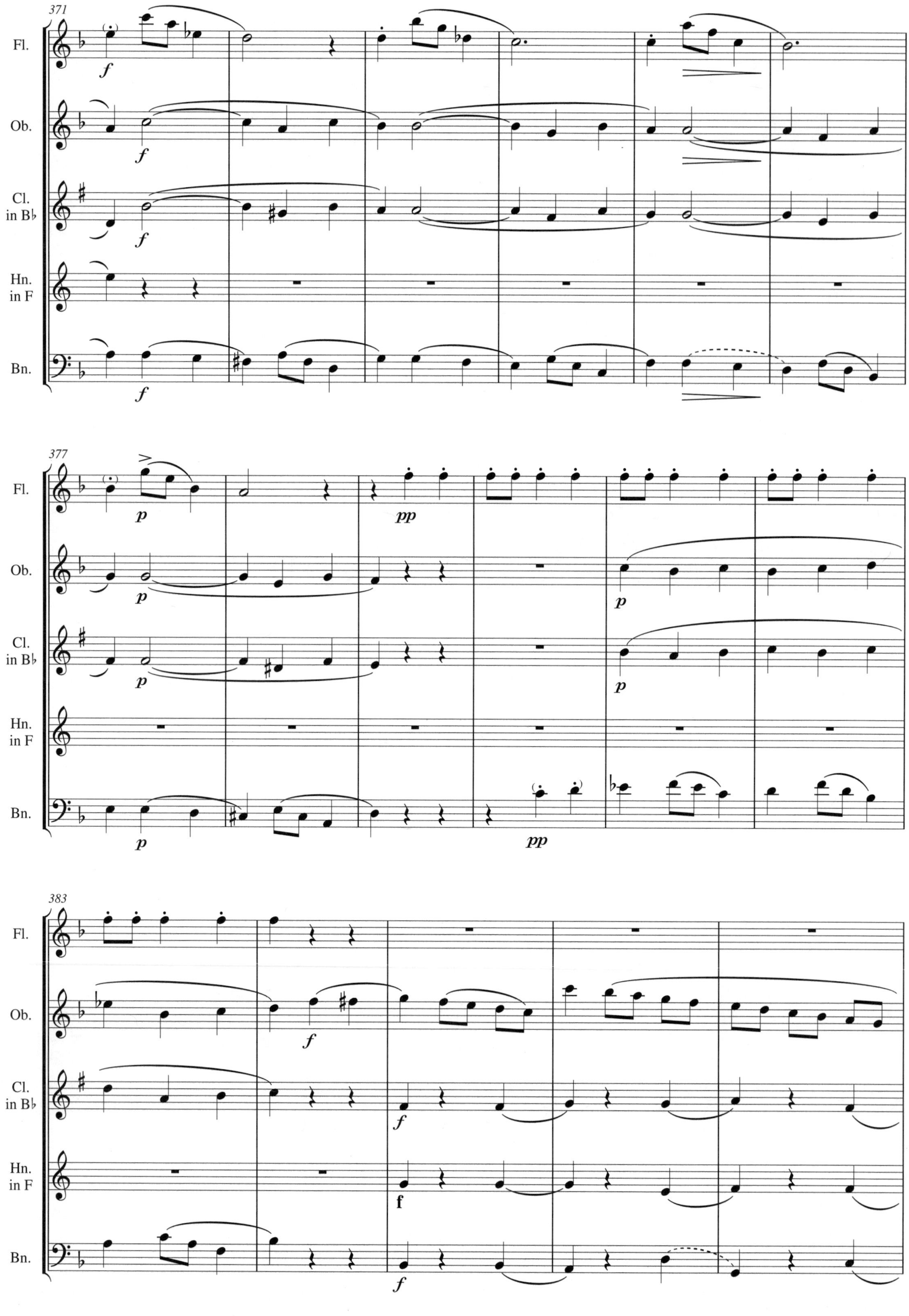
371
Fl.
Ob.
Cl.
in B♭
Hn.
in F
Bn.
f
377
p
pp
383
f

23

406
Fl.
Ob.
Cl. in B♭
Hn. in F
Bn.
sf
sf
sf
sf
411
Fl.
Ob.
Cl. in B♭
Hn. in F
Bn.
417
Fl.
Ob.
Cl. in B♭
Hn. in F
Bn.

[II]

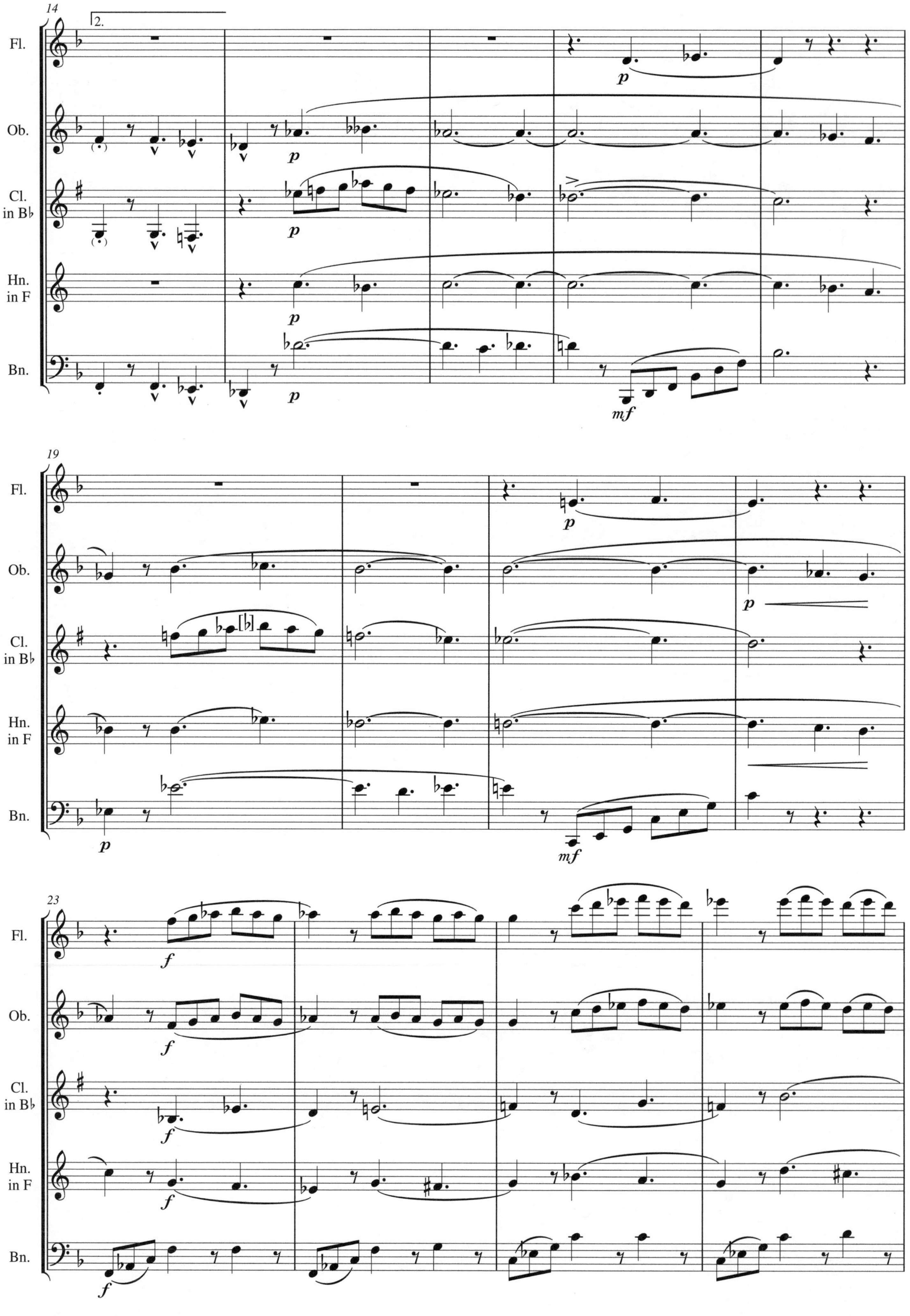
14
2.
Fl.
Ob.
Cl. in B♭
Hn. in F
Bn.
p
mf
19
23
f

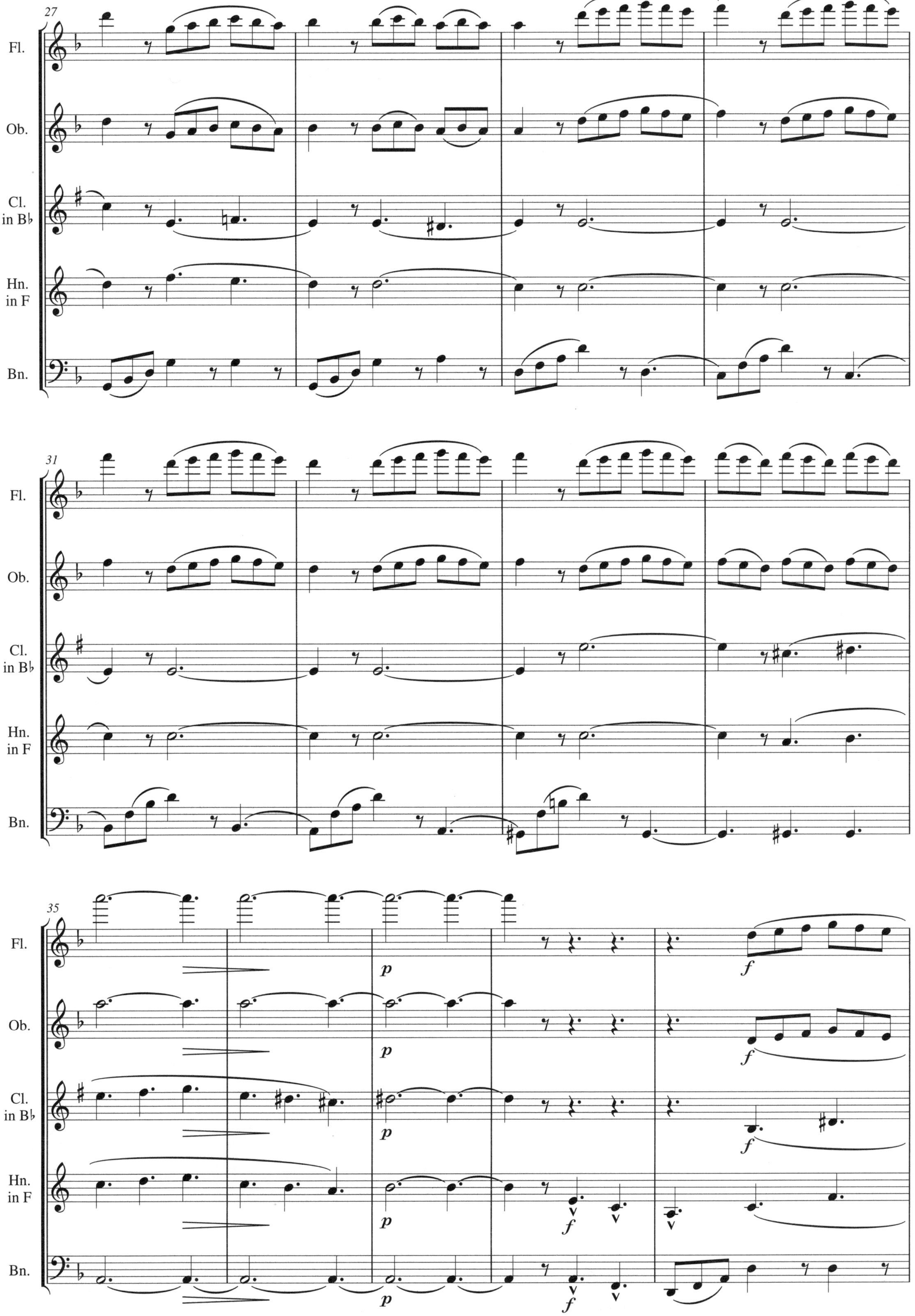
27
Fl.
Ob.
Cl. in B♭
Hn. in F
Bn.
31
35
p
f

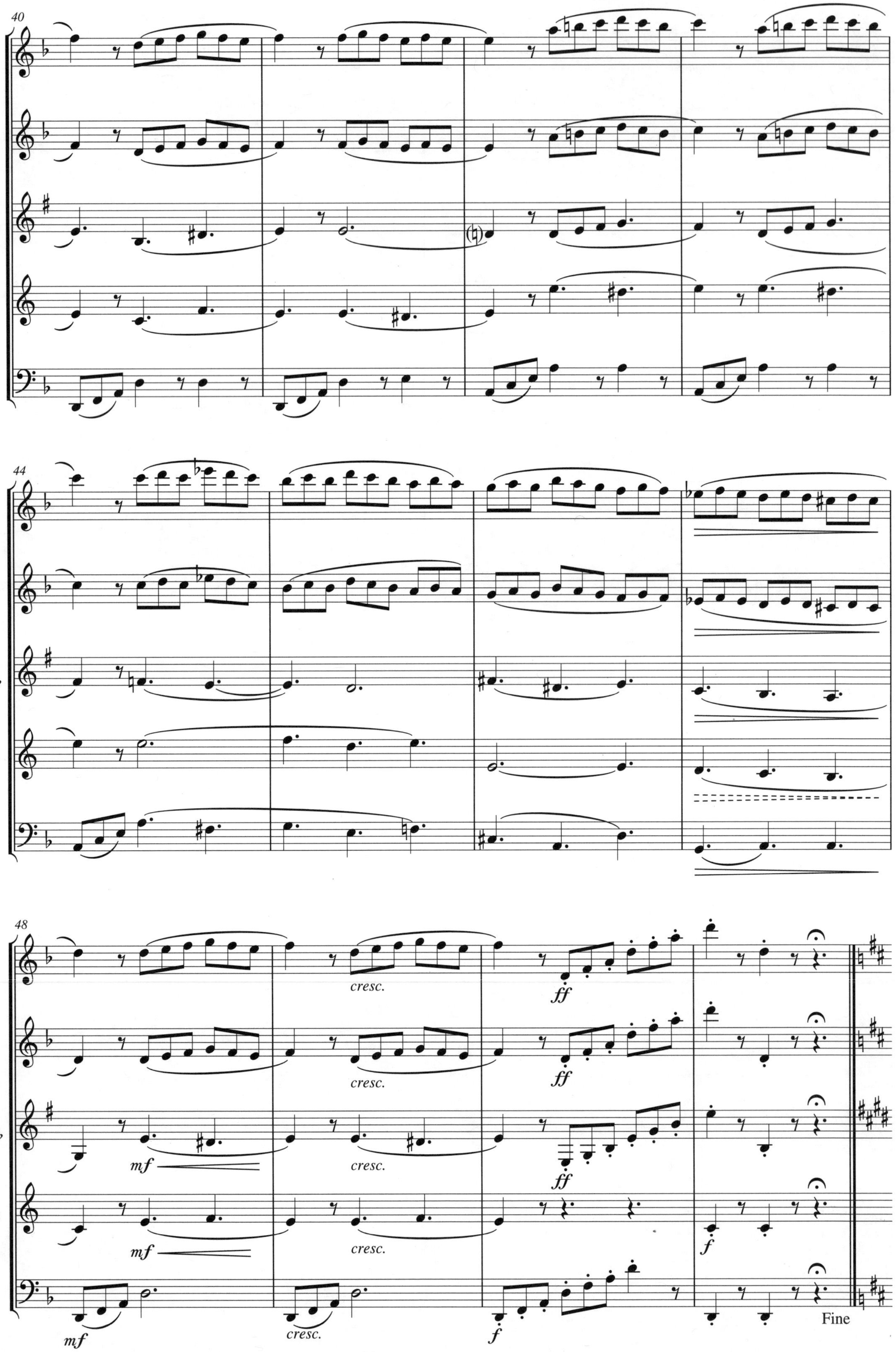
40
Fl.
Ob.
Cl. in B♭
Hn. in F
Bn.
44
48
cresc.
ff
mf
f
Fine

52
Trio
Fl.
Ob.
Cl. in B♭
Hn. in D
Bn.
pp
p
in D
56
p [sempre staccato]
p [sempre staccato]
60

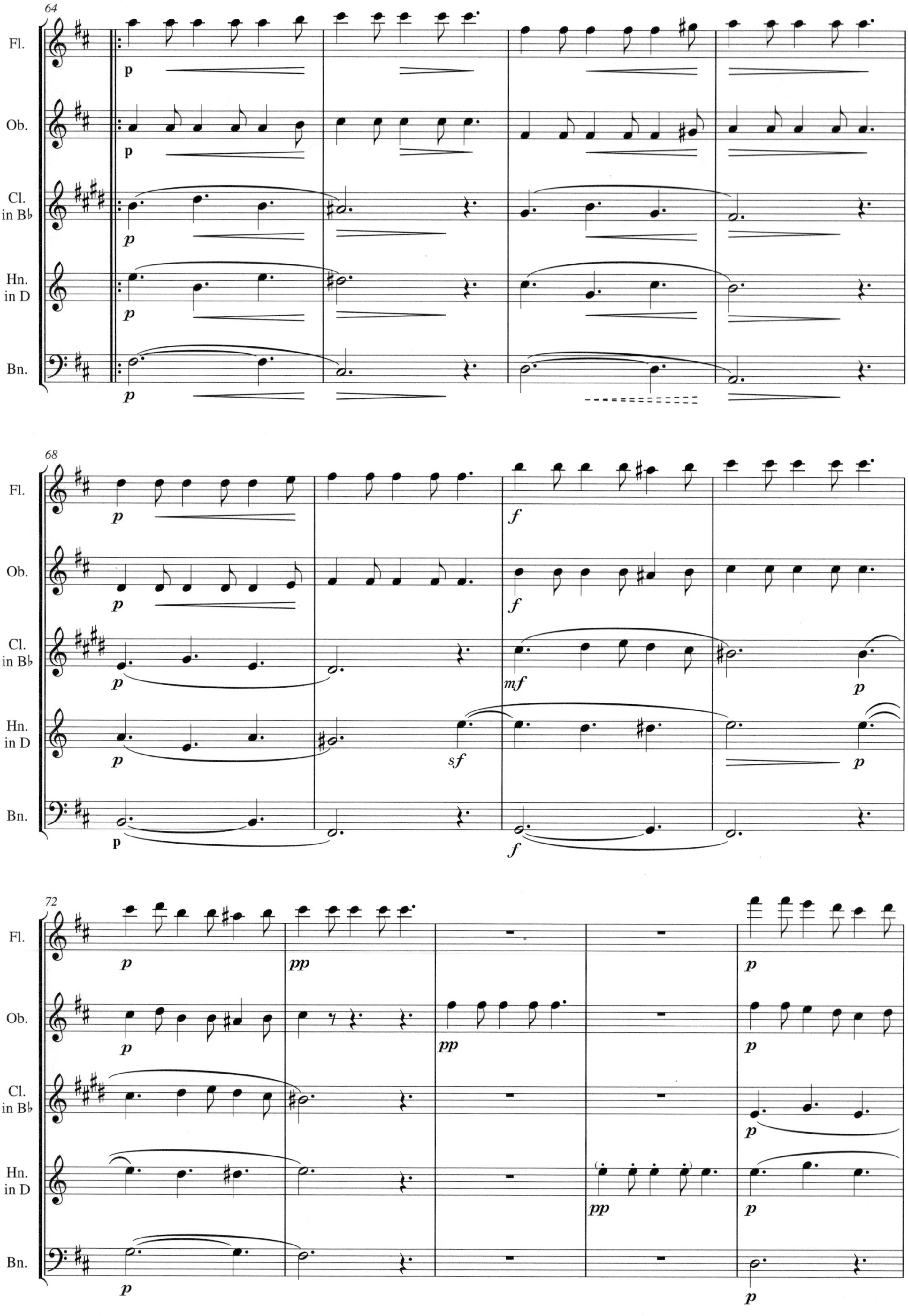
64
Fl.
Ob.
Cl. in B♭
Hn. in D
Bn.
p
68
f
mf
sf
72
pp

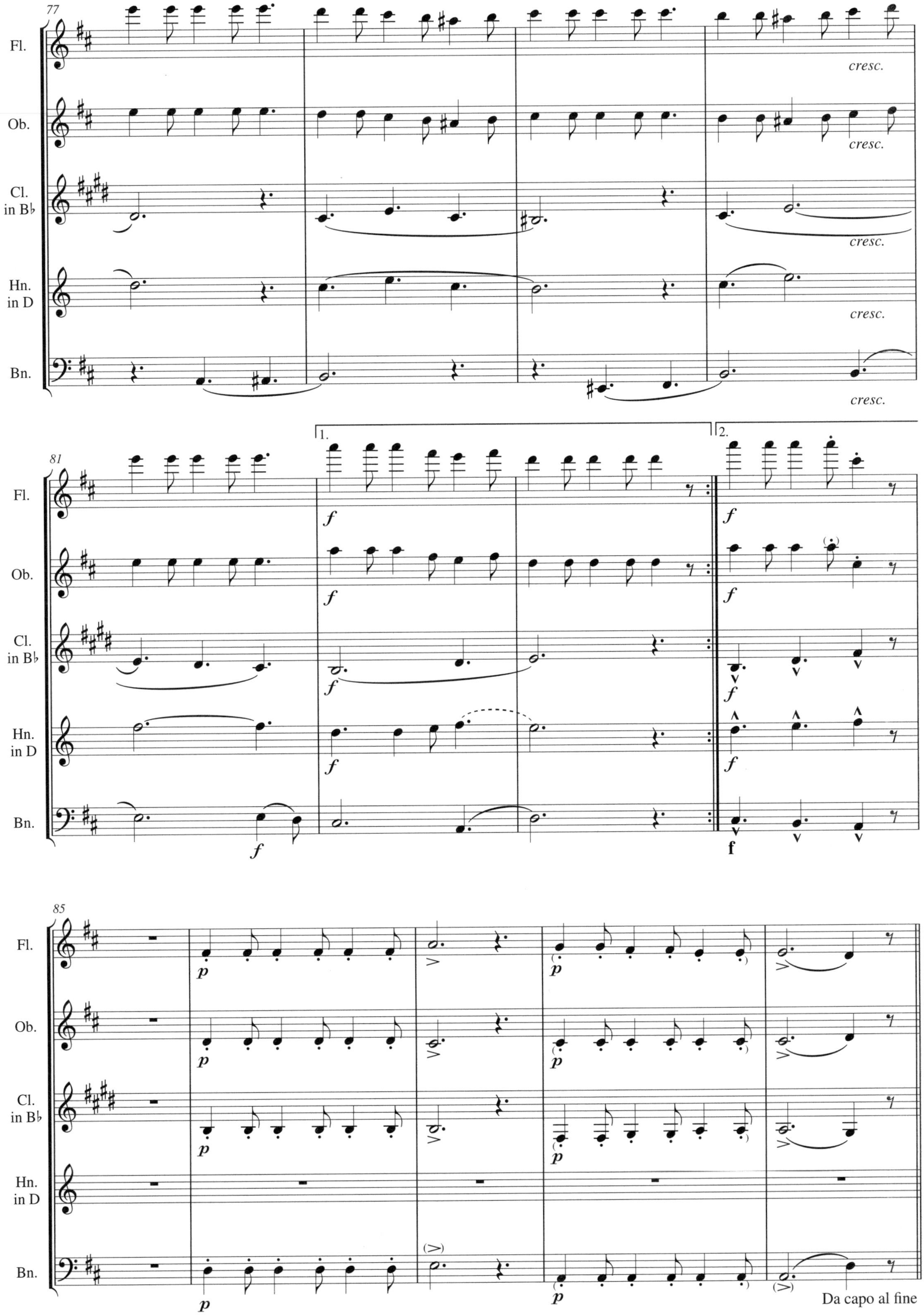
77
Fl.
Ob.
Cl. in B♭
Hn. in D
Bn.
cresc.
81
1.
2.
85
Da capo al fine

[III]

33

34

47
Fl.
Ob.
Cl. in B♭
Hn. in F
Bn.
p
51
tr
55
sempre staccato
[sempre staccato]
mf

36

71
Fl.
Ob.
Cl. in B♭
Hn. in F
Bn.
tr
p
75
sempre staccato
[sempre staccato]
mf
79
Allegro
fp [sempre staccato]

38

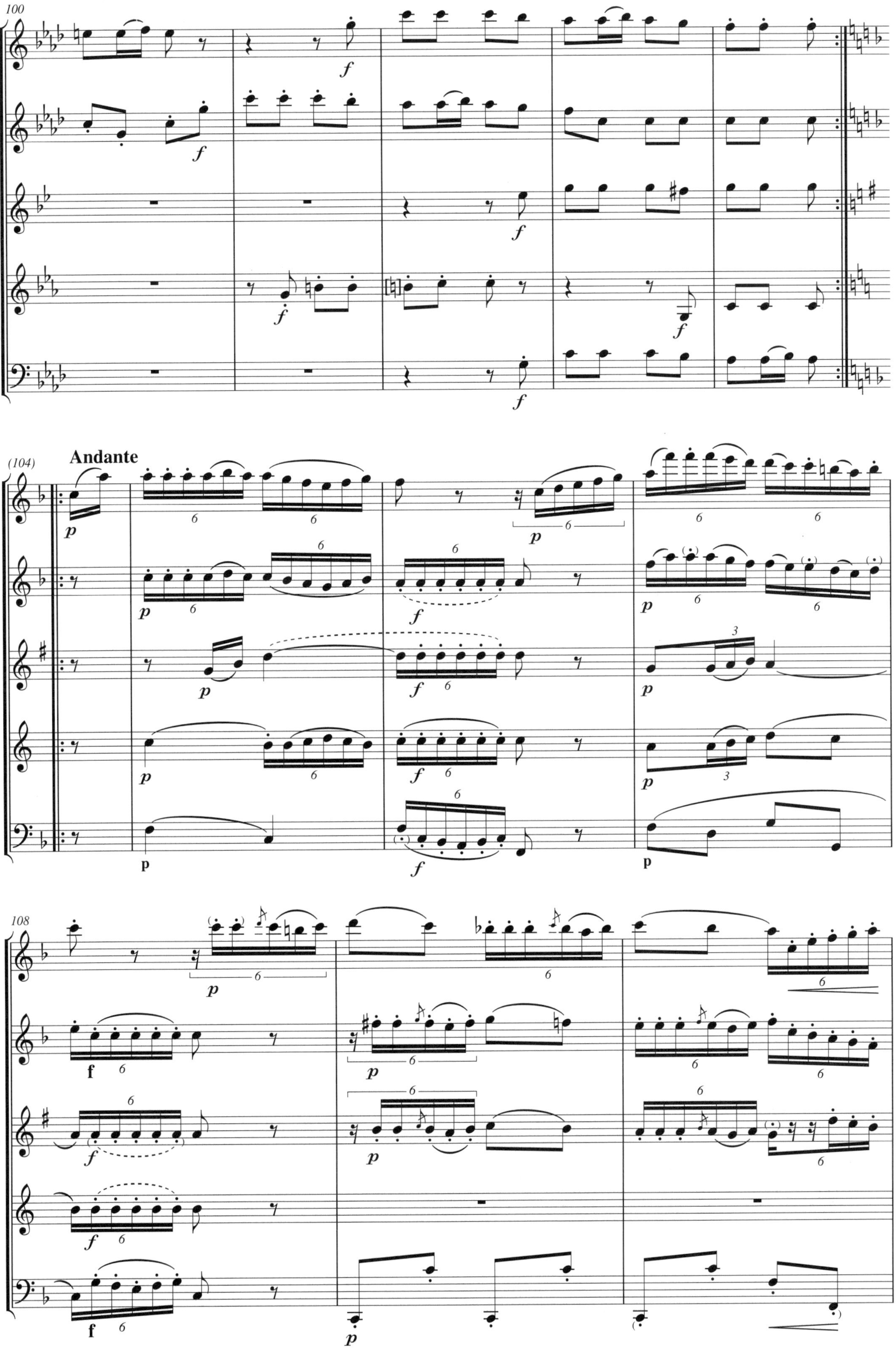
100
Fl.
Ob.
Cl. in B♭
Hn. in F
Bn.
(104)
Andante
108

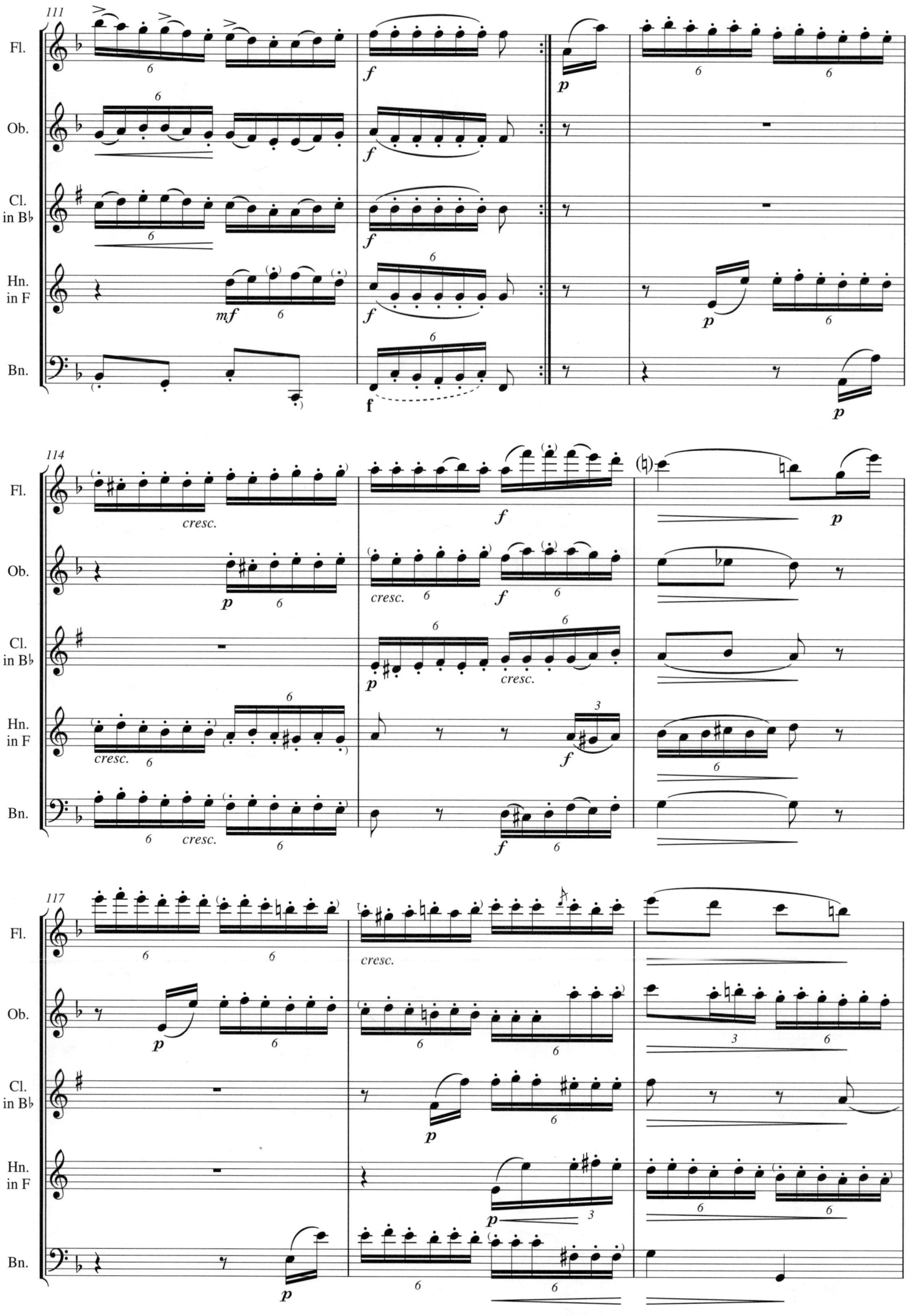
111
Fl.
Ob.
Cl. in B♭
Hn. in F
Bn.
f
p
mf
114
cresc.
117

41

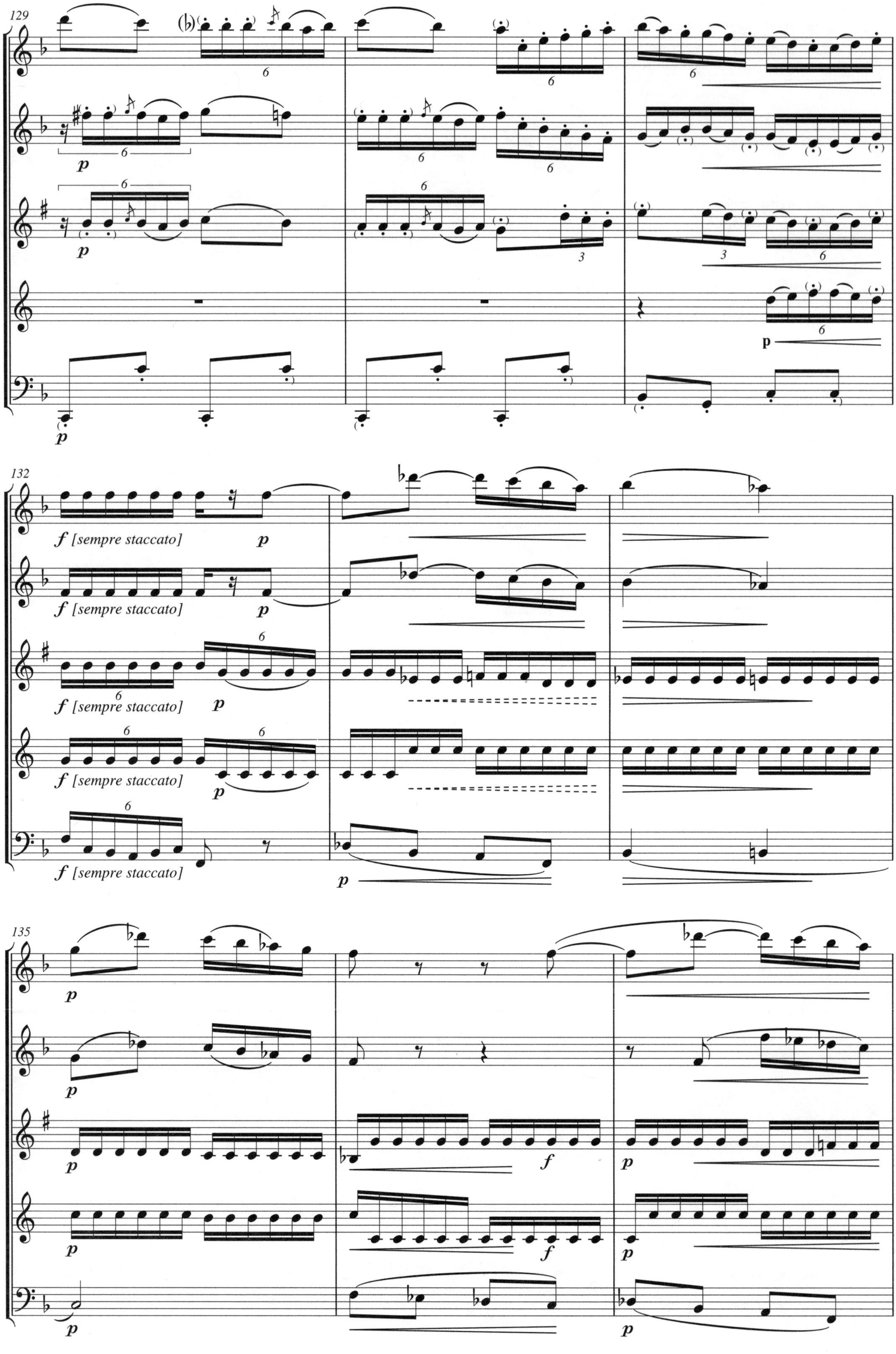
129
Fl.
Ob.
Cl. in B♭
Hn. in F
Bn.
132
f [sempre staccato]
135

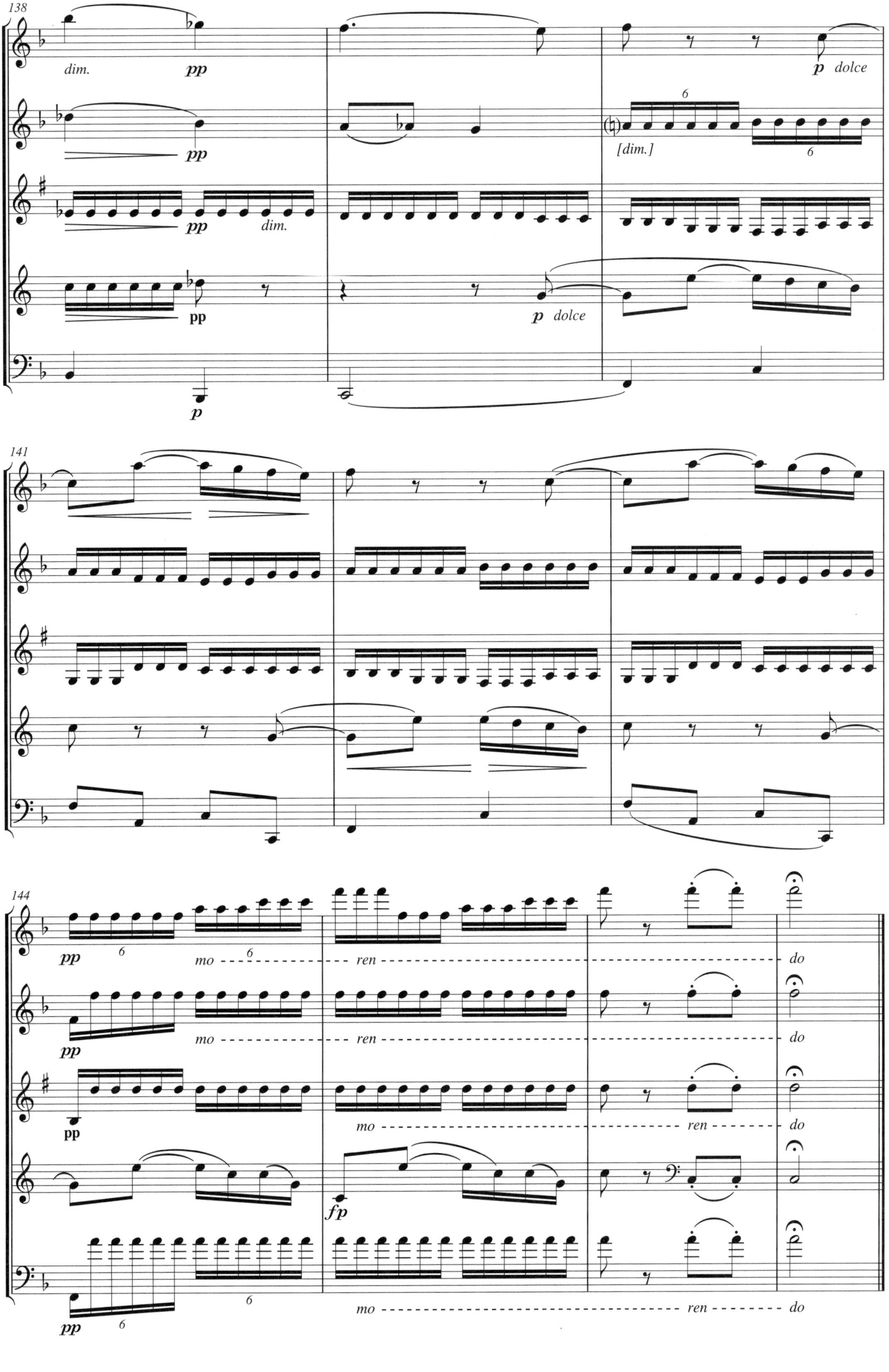
138
Fl.
Ob.
Cl. in B♭
Hn. in F
Bn.
dim.
pp
p dolce
[dim.]
dim.
p
141
144
mo
ren
do
fp

[IV]

Allegro

45

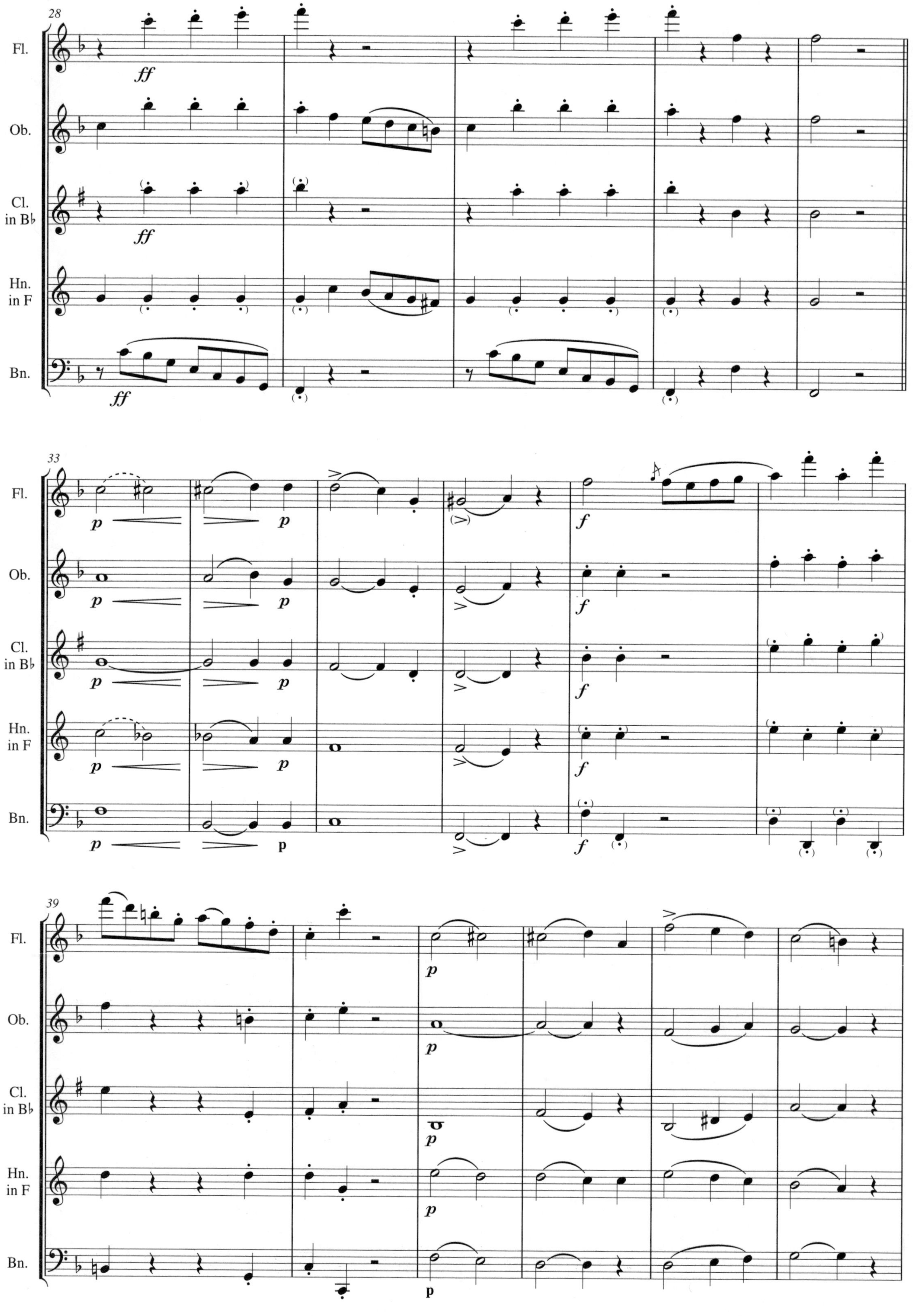
28
Fl.
Ob.
Cl. in B♭
Hn. in F
Bn.
ff
33
p
f
39

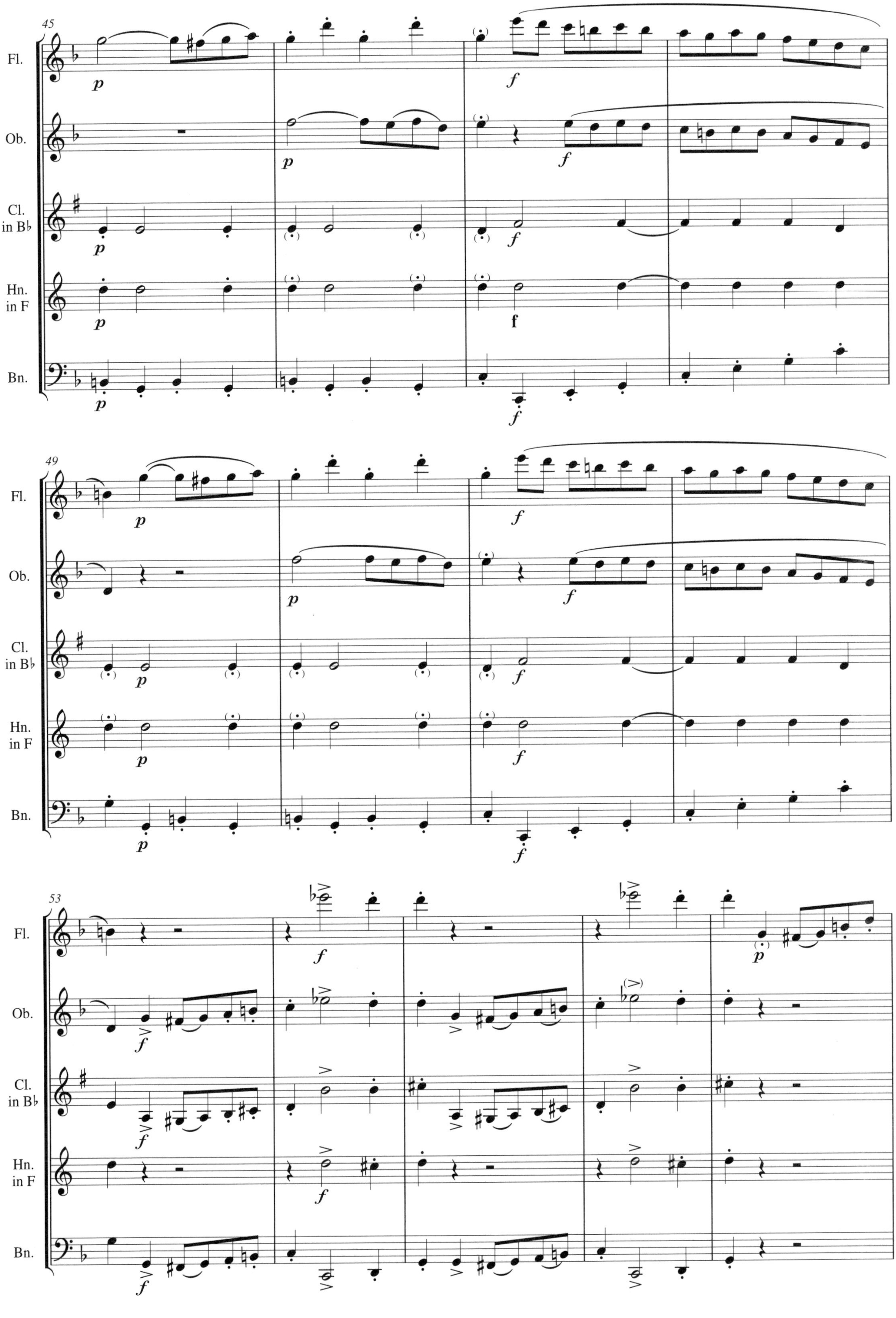
45
Fl.
Ob.
Cl. in B♭
Hn. in F
Bn.
49
53

58
Fl.
Ob.
Cl. in B♭
Hn. in F
Bn.
pp
dim.
p dolce
p
p
p
p
63
Fl.
Ob.
Cl. in B♭
Hn. in F
Bn.
3
3
3
3
68
Fl.
Ob.
Cl. in B♭
Hn. in F
Bn.
[♯]

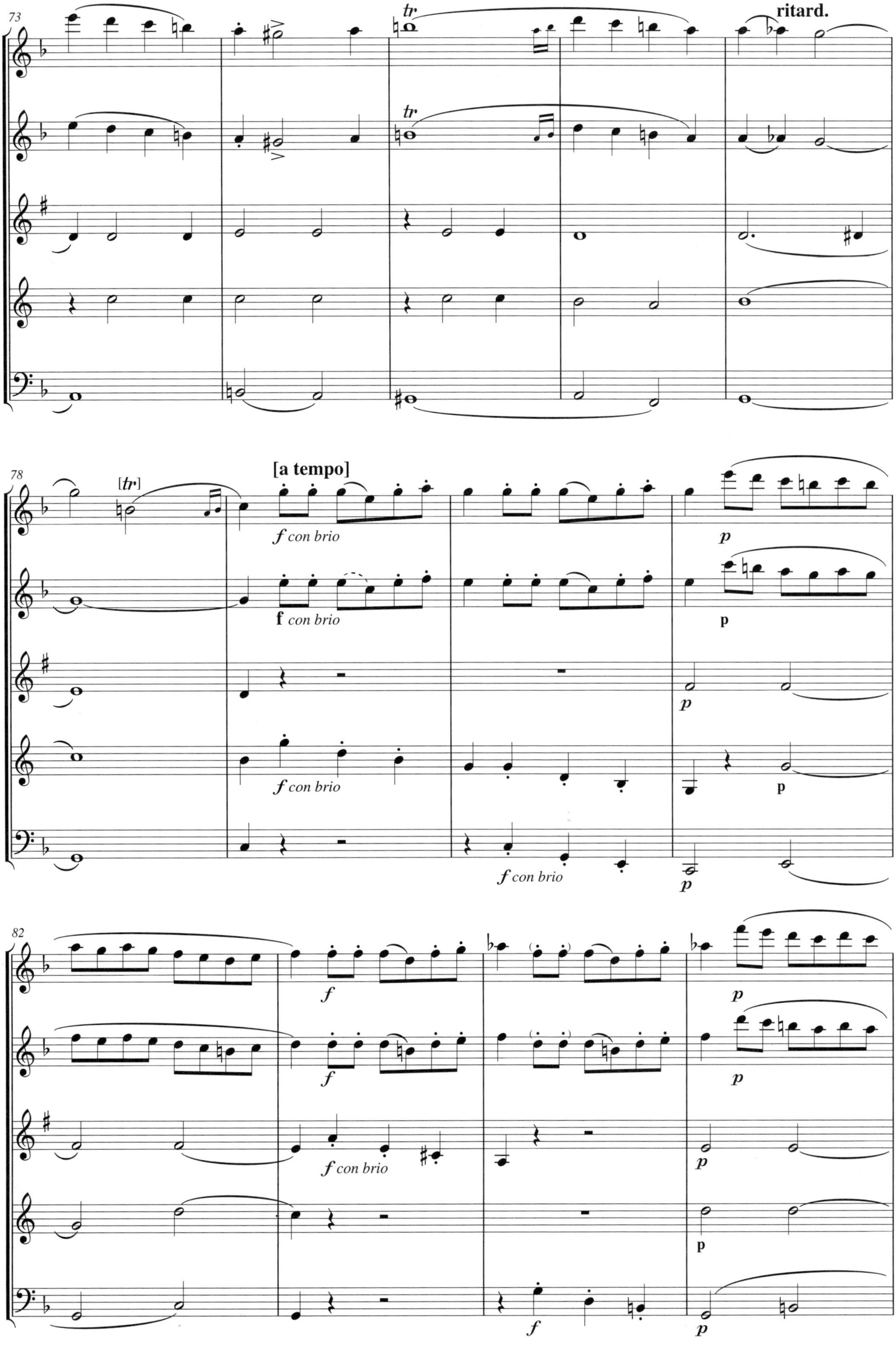
73
Fl.
Ob.
Cl. in B♭
Hn. in F
Bn.
tr
ritard.
78
[tr]
[a tempo]
f con brio
p
82
f

50

51

112
Fl.
Ob.
Cl. in B♭
Hn. in F
Bn.
cresc.
cresc.
cresc.
cresc.
cresc.
f
f
f
f
f
117
Fl.
Ob.
Cl. in B♭
Hn. in F
Bn.
p
p
121
Fl.
Ob.
Cl. in B♭
Hn. in F
Bn.
mf
cresc.
f
cresc.
f
p
cresc.
f
cresc.
f
f

125
Fl.
Ob.
Cl.
in B♭
Hn.
in F
Bn.
129
Fl.
Ob.
Cl.
in B♭
Hn.
in F
Bn.
134
Fl.
Ob.
Cl.
in B♭
Hn.
in F
Bn.

54

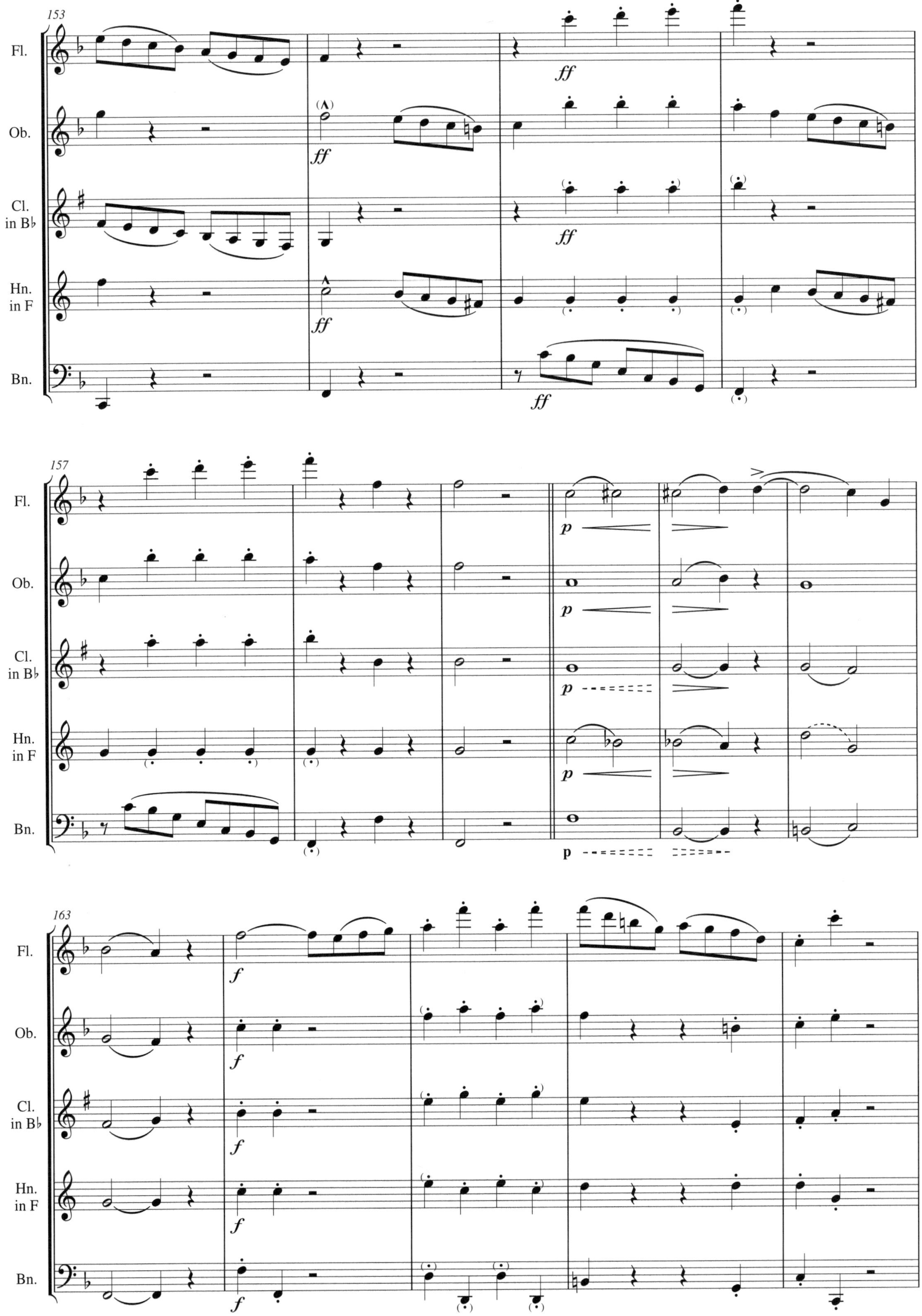
153
Fl.
Ob.
Cl. in B♭
Hn. in F
Bn.
ff
157
p
163
f

168
Fl.
Ob.
Cl. in B♭
Hn. in F
Bn.
174
Fl.
Ob.
Cl. in B♭
Hn. in F
Bn.
178
Fl.
Ob.
Cl. in B♭
Hn. in F
Bn.

57

199
Fl.
Ob.
Cl. in B♭
Hn. in F
Bn.
mf
p
f
tr
205
ritard.
[a tempo]
pp
f con brio
211
f

215
Fl.
Ob.
Cl. in B♭
Hn. in F
Bn.
219
Fl.
Ob.
Cl. in B♭
Hn. in F
Bn.
223
Fl.
Ob.
Cl. in B♭
Hn. in F
Bn.

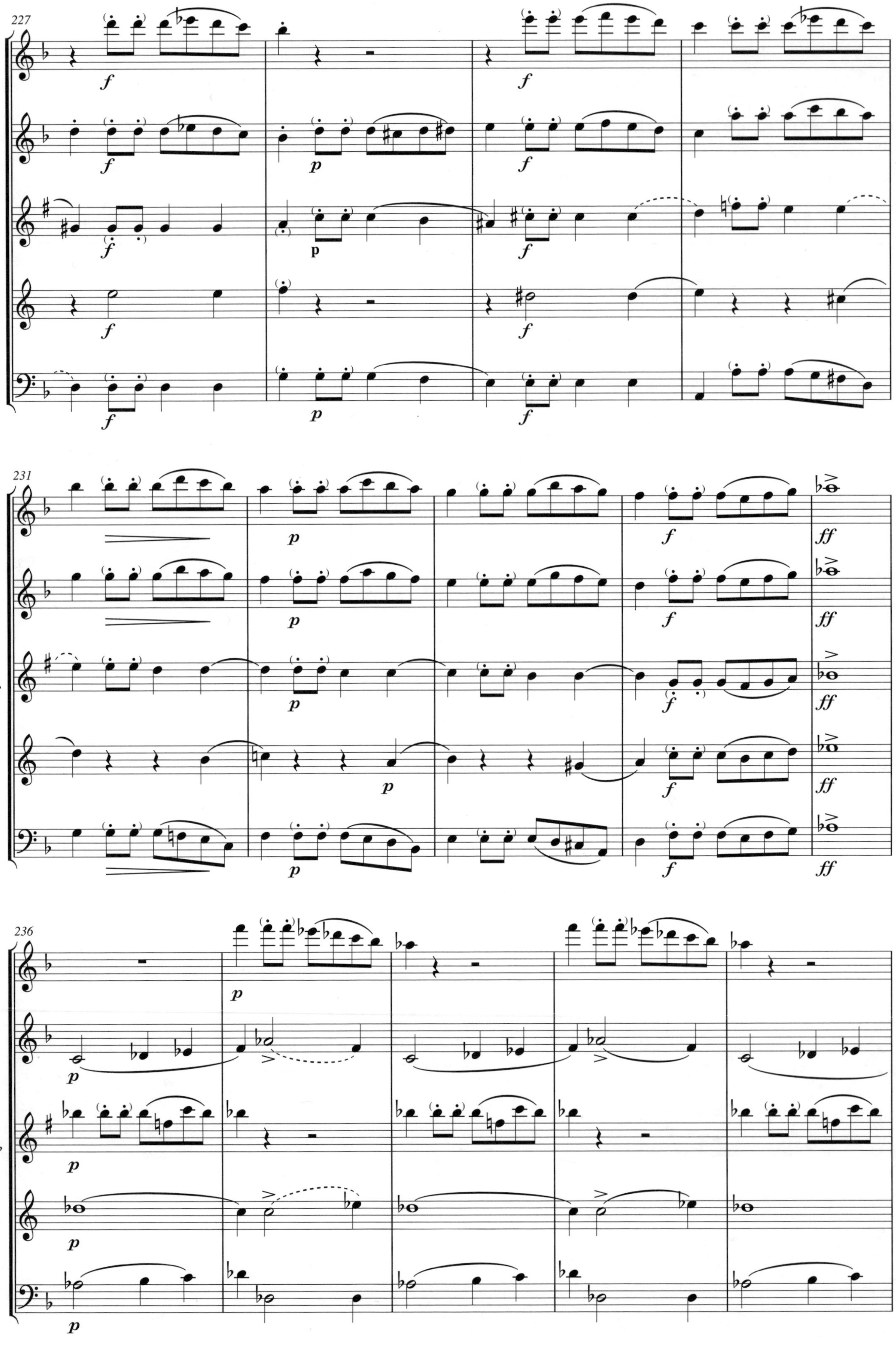
227
231
236
Fl.
Ob.
Cl. in B♭
Hn. in F
Bn.

61

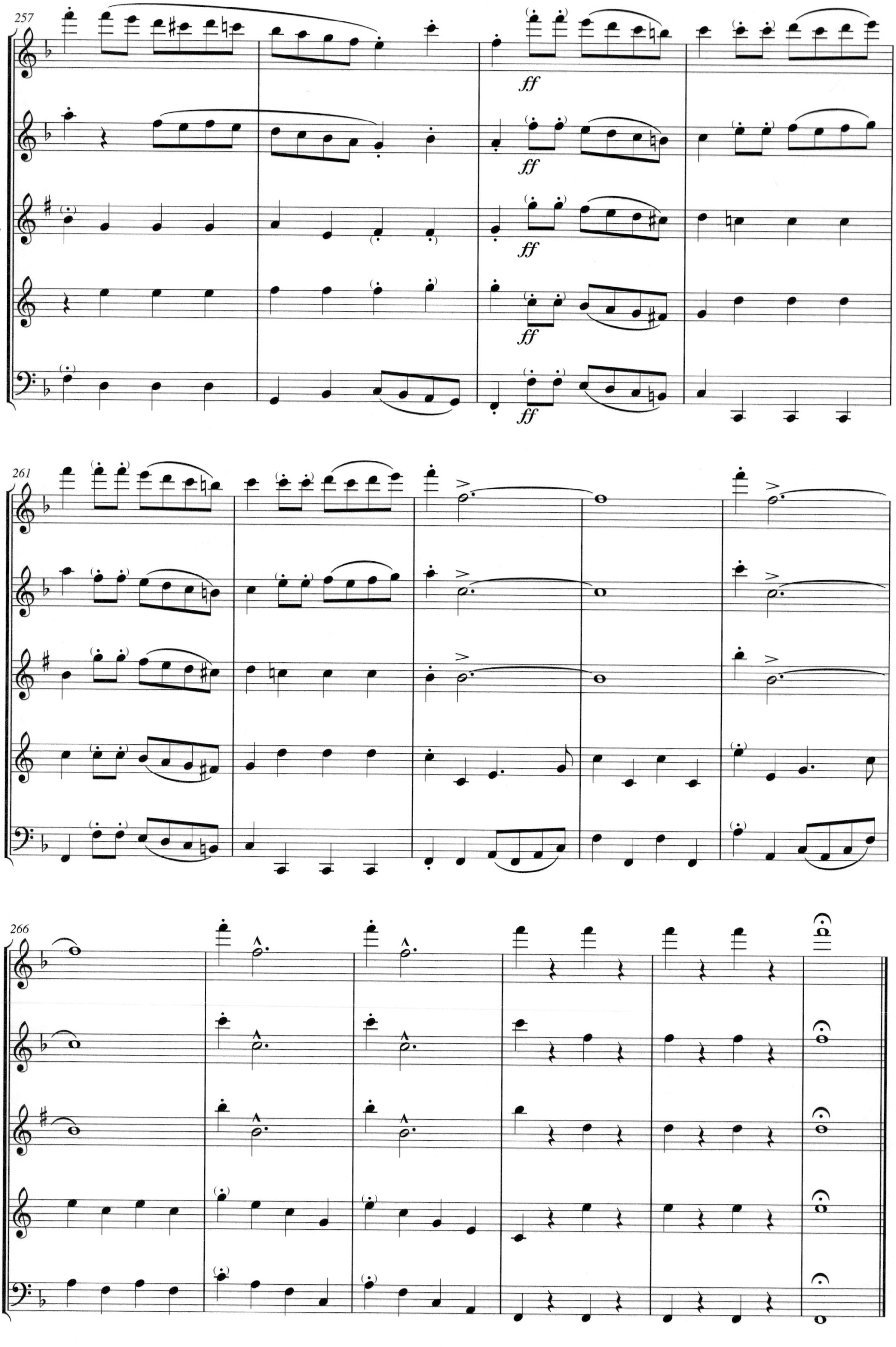
257
Fl.
Ob.
Cl. in B♭
Hn. in F
Bn.
ff
261
266

Woodwind Quintet No. 2 in E-flat Major

[I]

*This passage is omitted in the autograph manuscript; for a discussion of the issue, see the editorial method section under "Erasures."

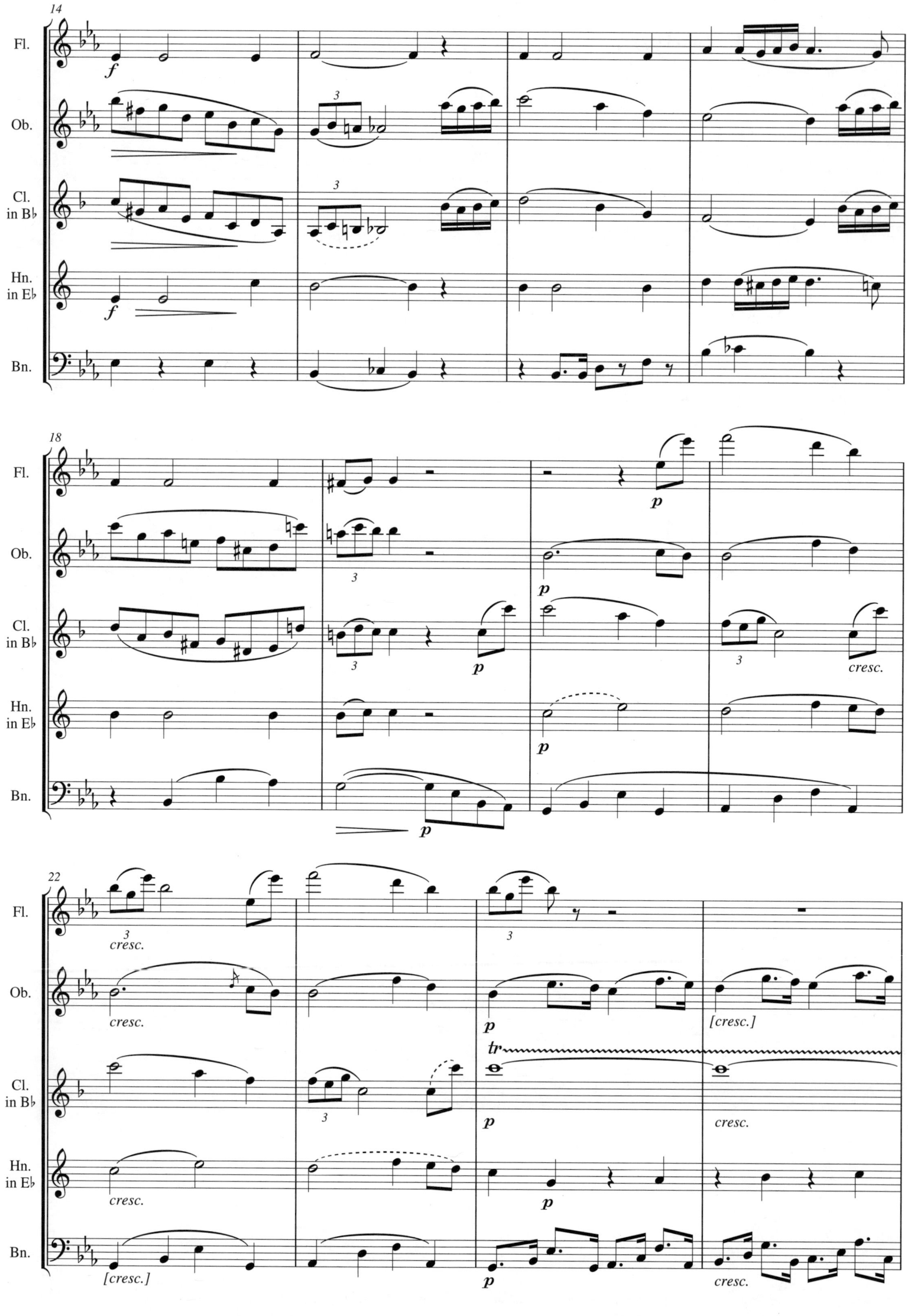
14
Fl.
Ob.
Cl. in B♭
Hn. in E♭
Bn.
18
cresc.
22
[cresc.]

65

40
Fl.
Ob.
Cl. in B♭
Hn. in E♭
Bn.
cresc.
cresc.
cresc.
cresc.
f
f
f
f
44
fp
fp
fp
fp
f
f
48
f
p
f

52
Fl.
Ob.
Cl. in B♭
Hn. in E♭
Bn.
p
dim.
pp
56
Fl.
Ob.
Cl. in B♭
Hn. in E♭
Bn.
pp
pp
dolce
pp
pp
60
Fl.
Ob.
Cl. in B♭
Hn. in E♭
Bn.
cresc.
cresc.
cresc.
[cresc.]

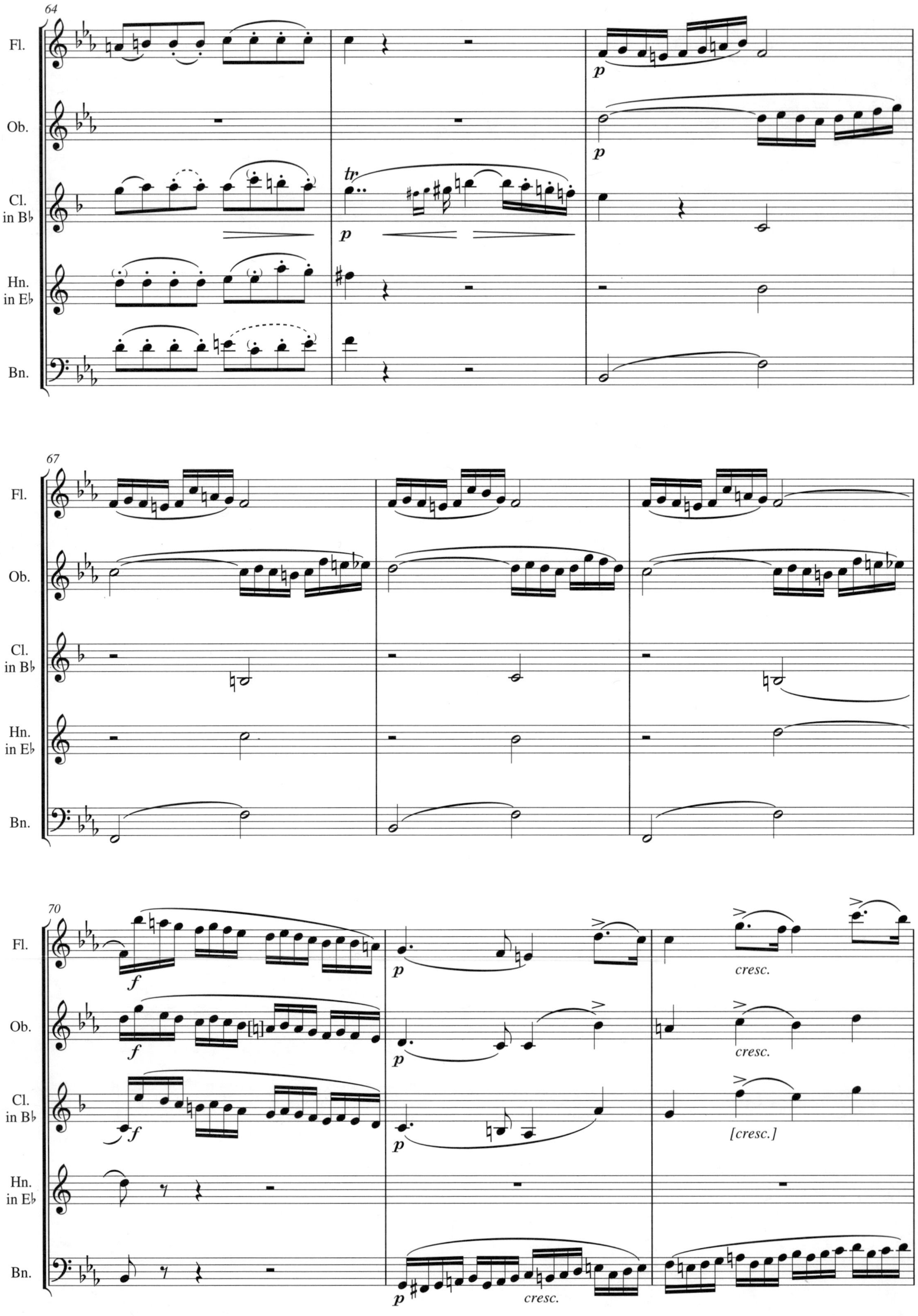
64
Fl.
Ob.
Cl.
in B♭
Hn.
in E♭
Bn.
tr
p
67
70
f
cresc.
[cresc.]

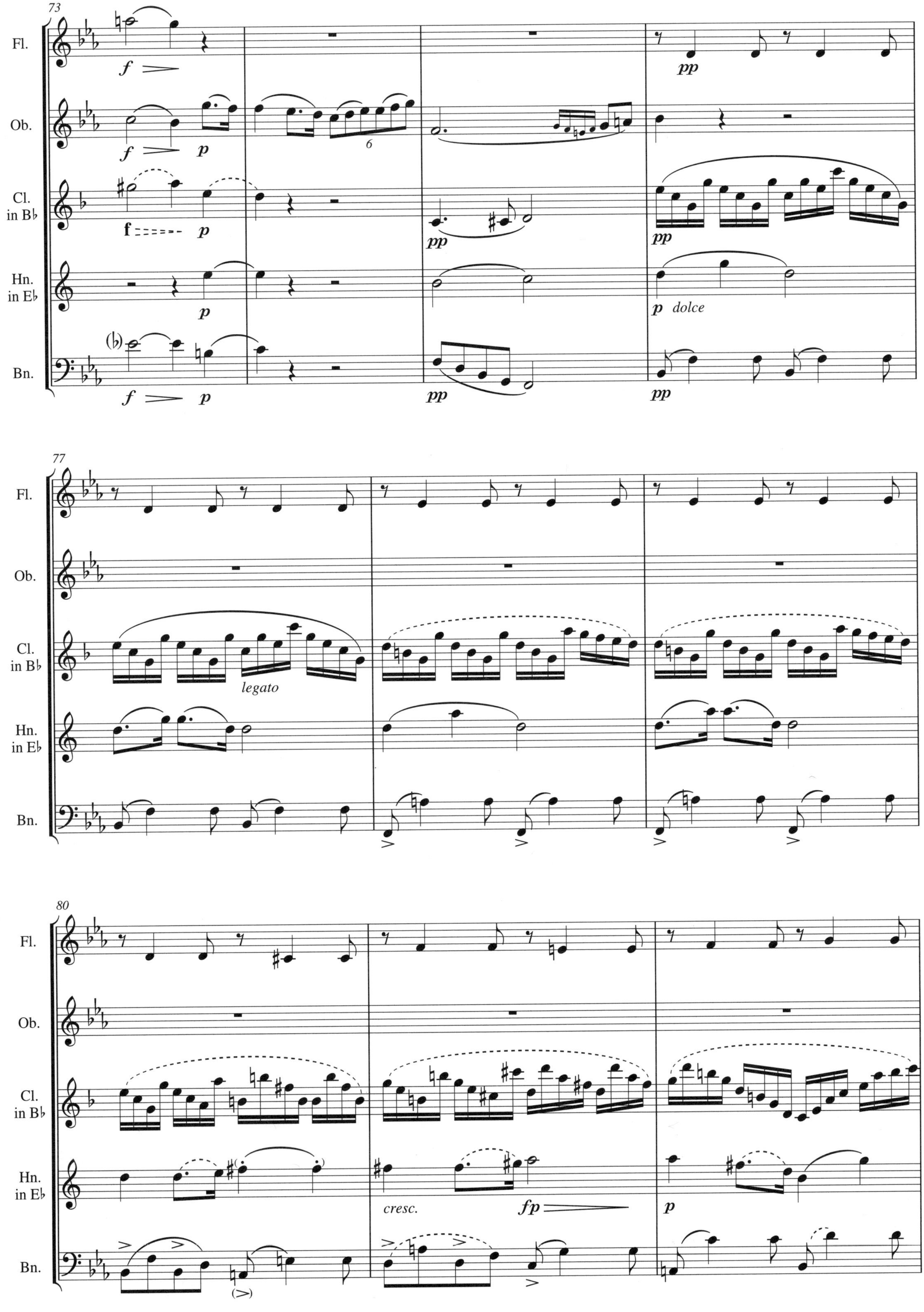
73
Fl.
Ob.
Cl. in B♭
Hn. in E♭
Bn.
f
p
pp
dolce
6
77
legato
80
cresc.
fp

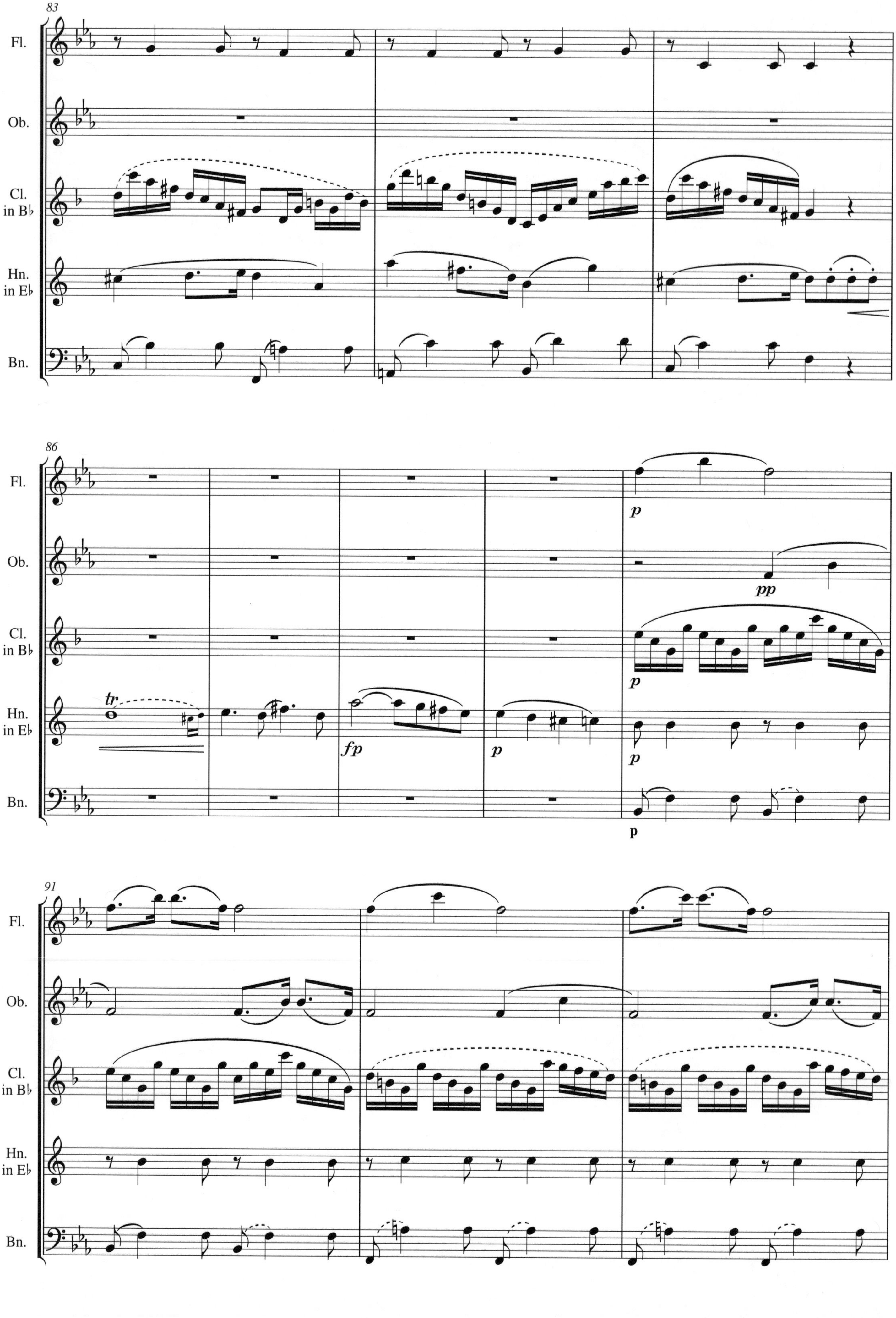
83
Fl.
Ob.
Cl. in B♭
Hn. in E♭
Bn.
86
p
pp
p
tr
fp
p
p
p
91

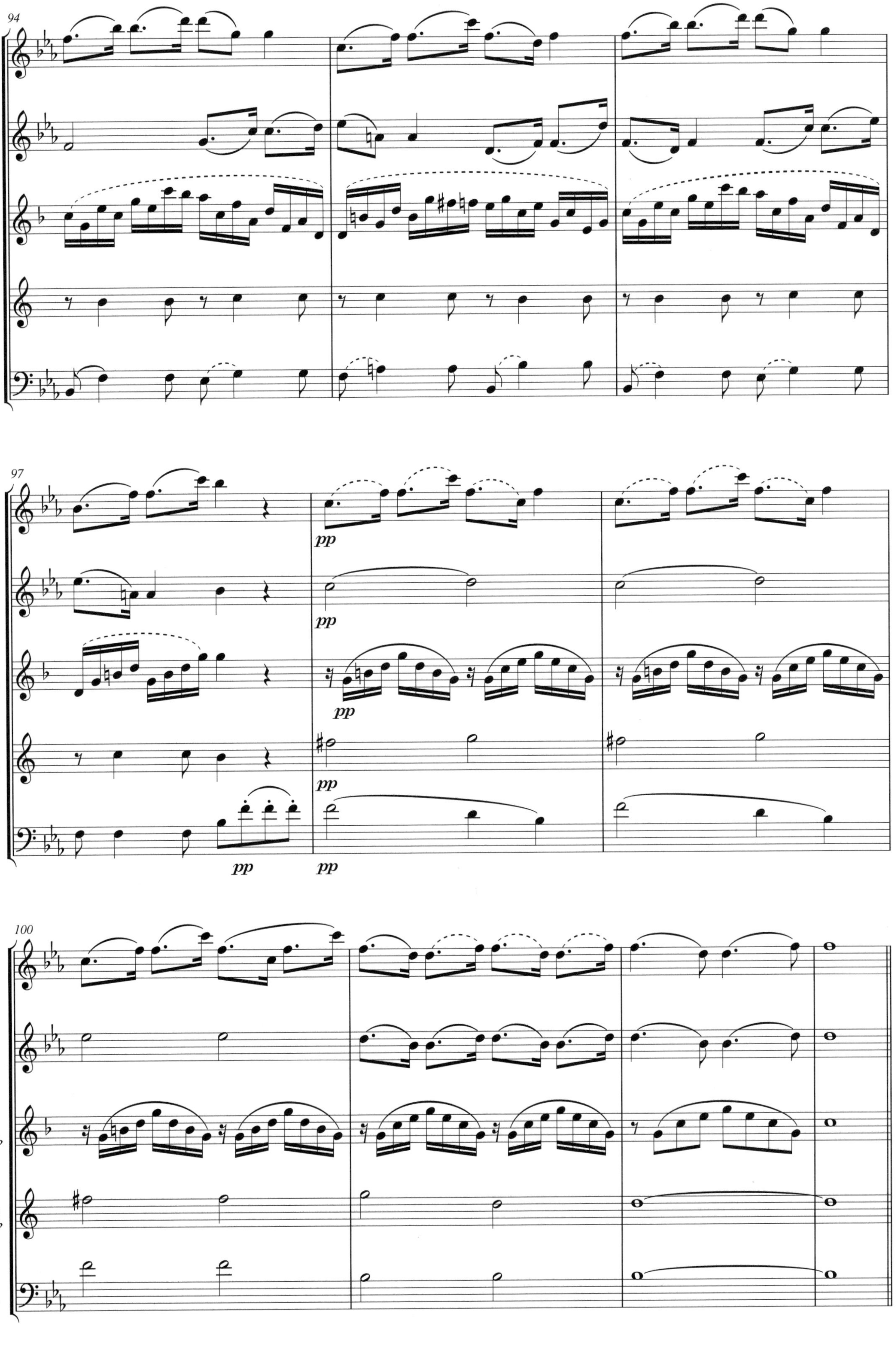
94
Fl.
Ob.
Cl. in B♭
Hn. in E♭
Bn.
97
pp
100

72

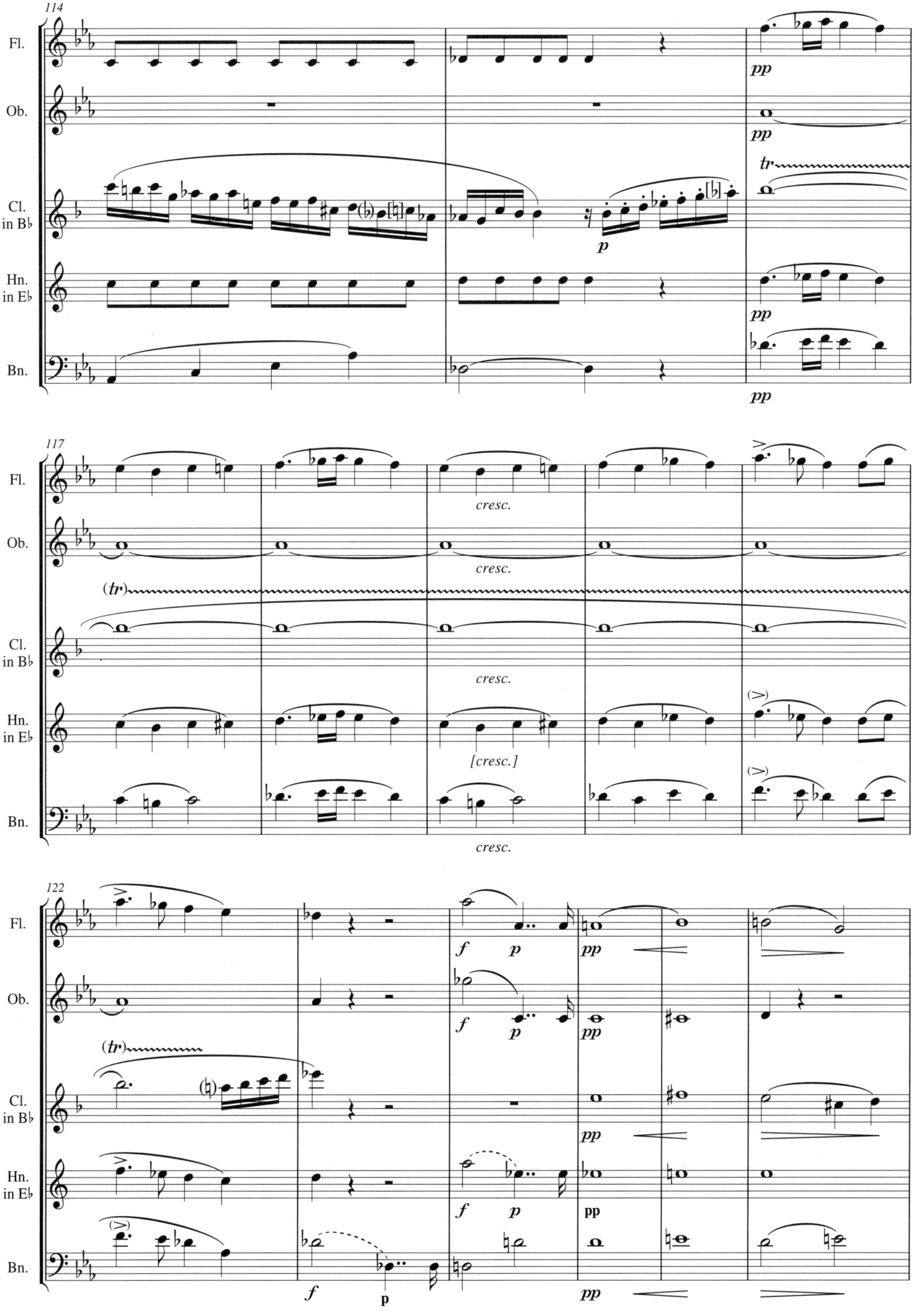
114
Fl.
Ob.
Cl. in B♭
Hn. in E♭
Bn.
pp
tr
p
117
cresc.
(tr)
[cresc.]
122
f
pp

74

75

76

77

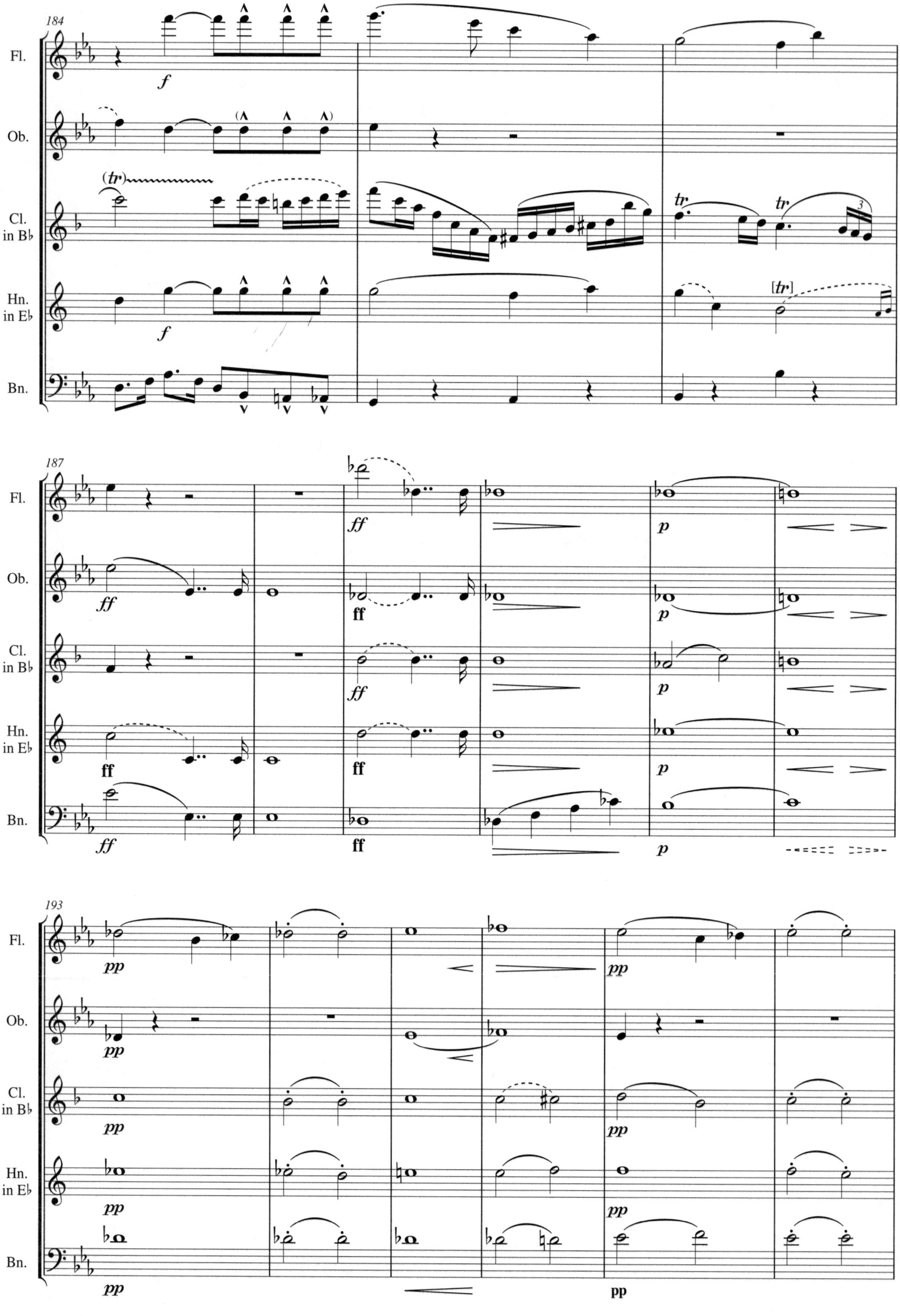
184
Fl.
Ob.
Cl.
in B♭
Hn.
in E♭
Bn.
f
(tr)
tr
[tr]
187
ff
p
193
pp

79

213
Fl.
Ob.
Cl. in B♭
Hn. in E♭
Bn.
218
Fl.
Ob.
Cl. in B♭
Hn. in E♭
Bn.
f
f
f
f
f
p
223
Fl.
Ob.
Cl. in B♭
Hn. in E♭
Bn.
fp
fp
f

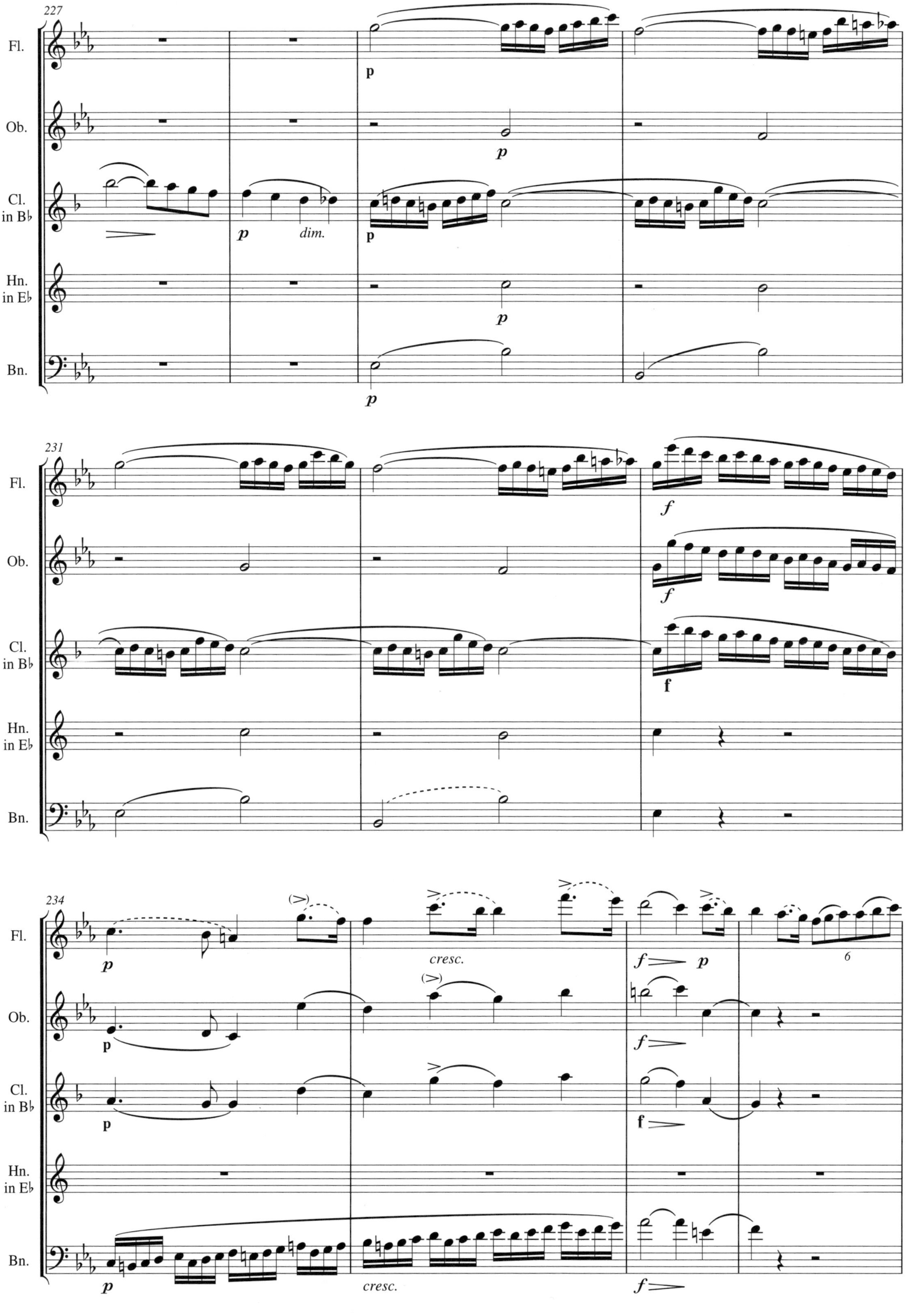
227
Fl.
Ob.
Cl. in B♭
Hn. in E♭
Bn.
dim.
231
234
cresc.
6

238
Fl.
Ob.
Cl.
in B♭
Hn.
in E♭
Bn.
pp
p
p
pp
p dolce
p
pp
241
Fl.
Ob.
Cl.
in B♭
Hn.
in E♭
Bn.
p
244
Fl.
Ob.
cresc.
Cl.
in B♭
Hn.
in E♭
pp
Bn.

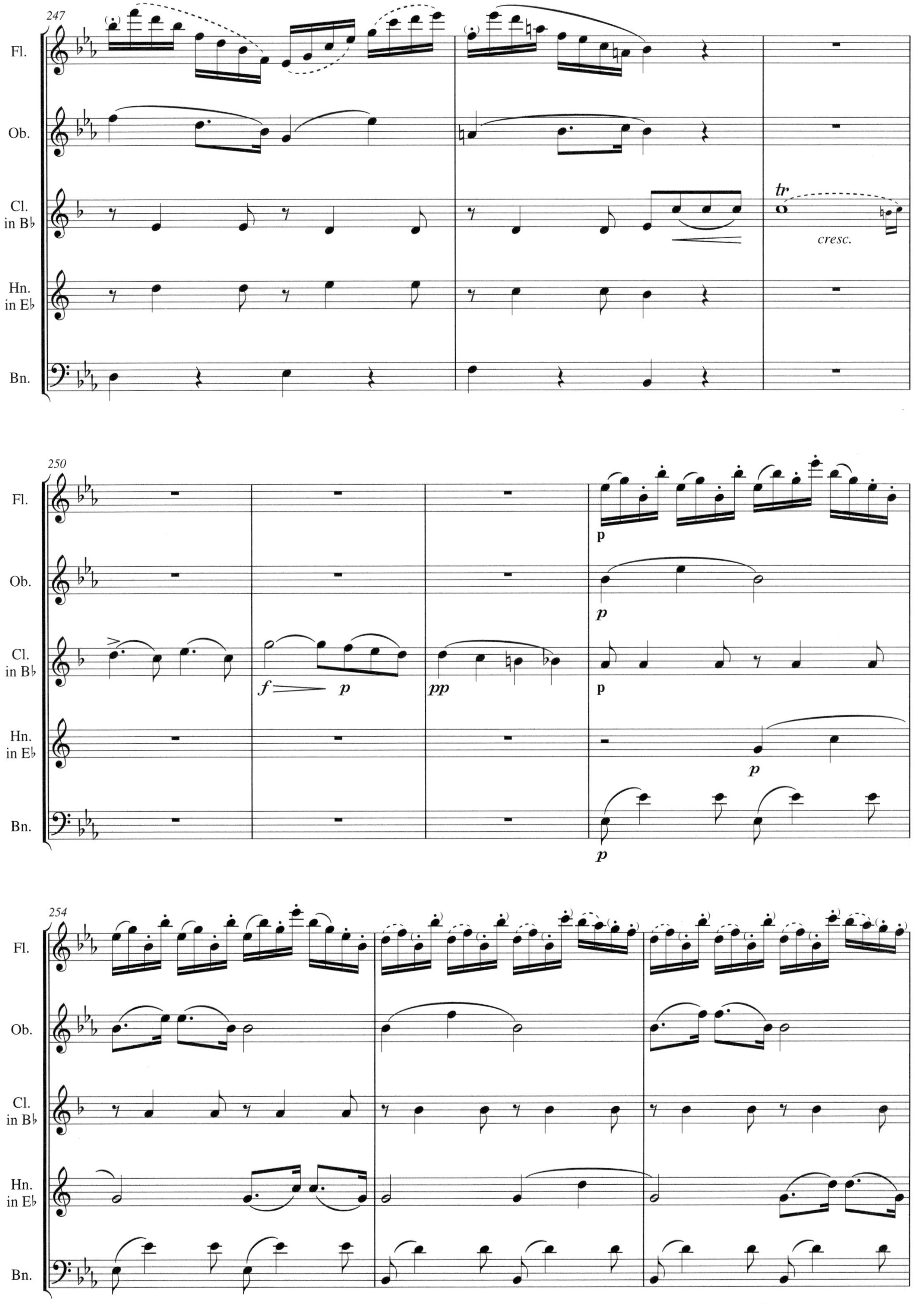
247
Fl.
Ob.
Cl. in B♭
Hn. in E♭
Bn.
tr
cresc.
250
f
p
pp
p
254

257
Fl.
Ob.
Cl. in B♭
Hn. in E♭
Bn.
260
Fl.
Ob.
Cl. in B♭
Hn. in E♭
Bn.
263
Fl.
p
cresc.
Ob.
p
cresc.
Cl. in B♭
p
cresc.
Hn. in E♭
p
Bn.
cresc.

85

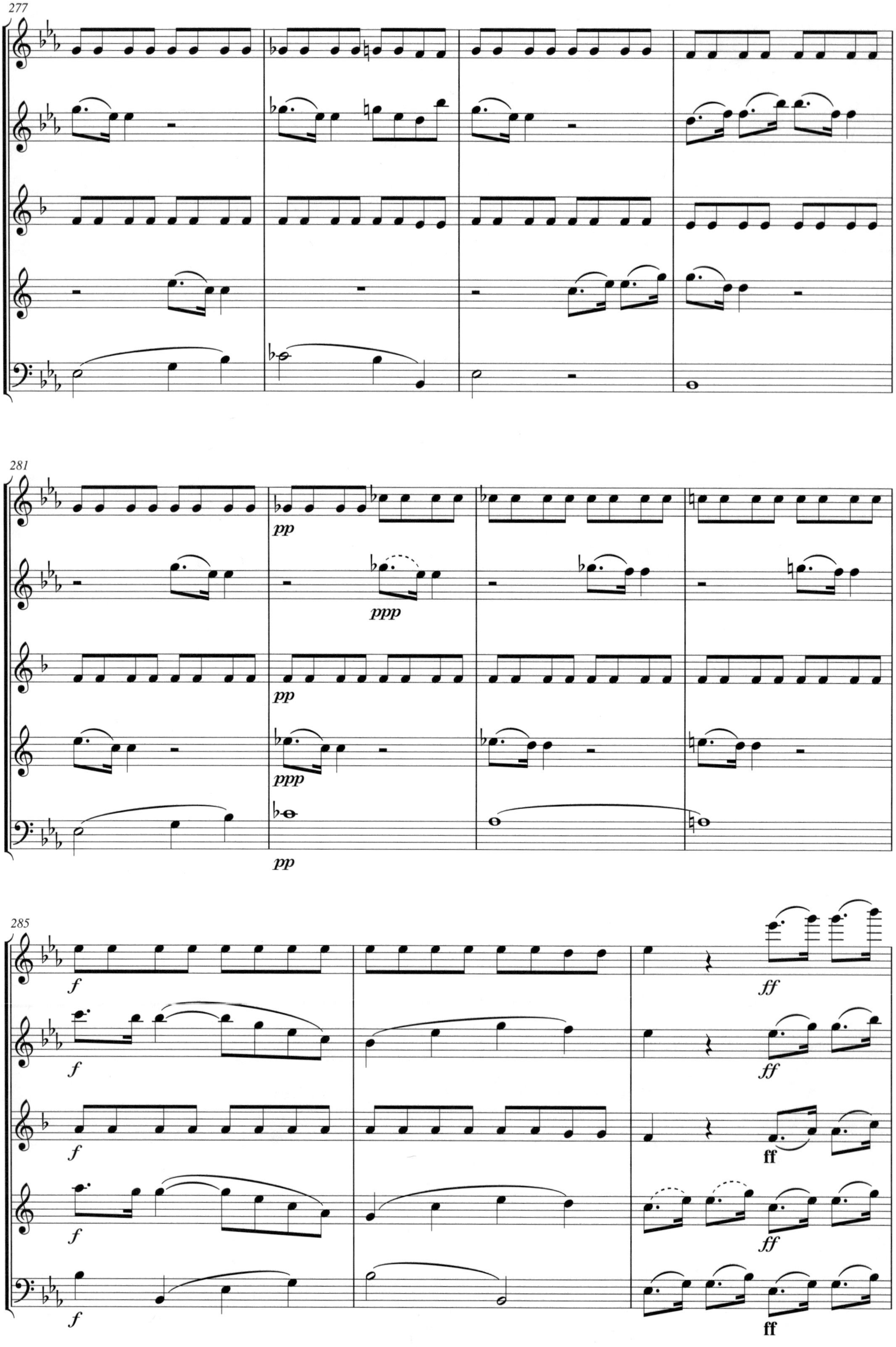
277
Fl.
Ob.
Cl. in B♭
Hn. in E♭
Bn.
281
pp
ppp
pp
ppp
pp
285
f
ff
ff

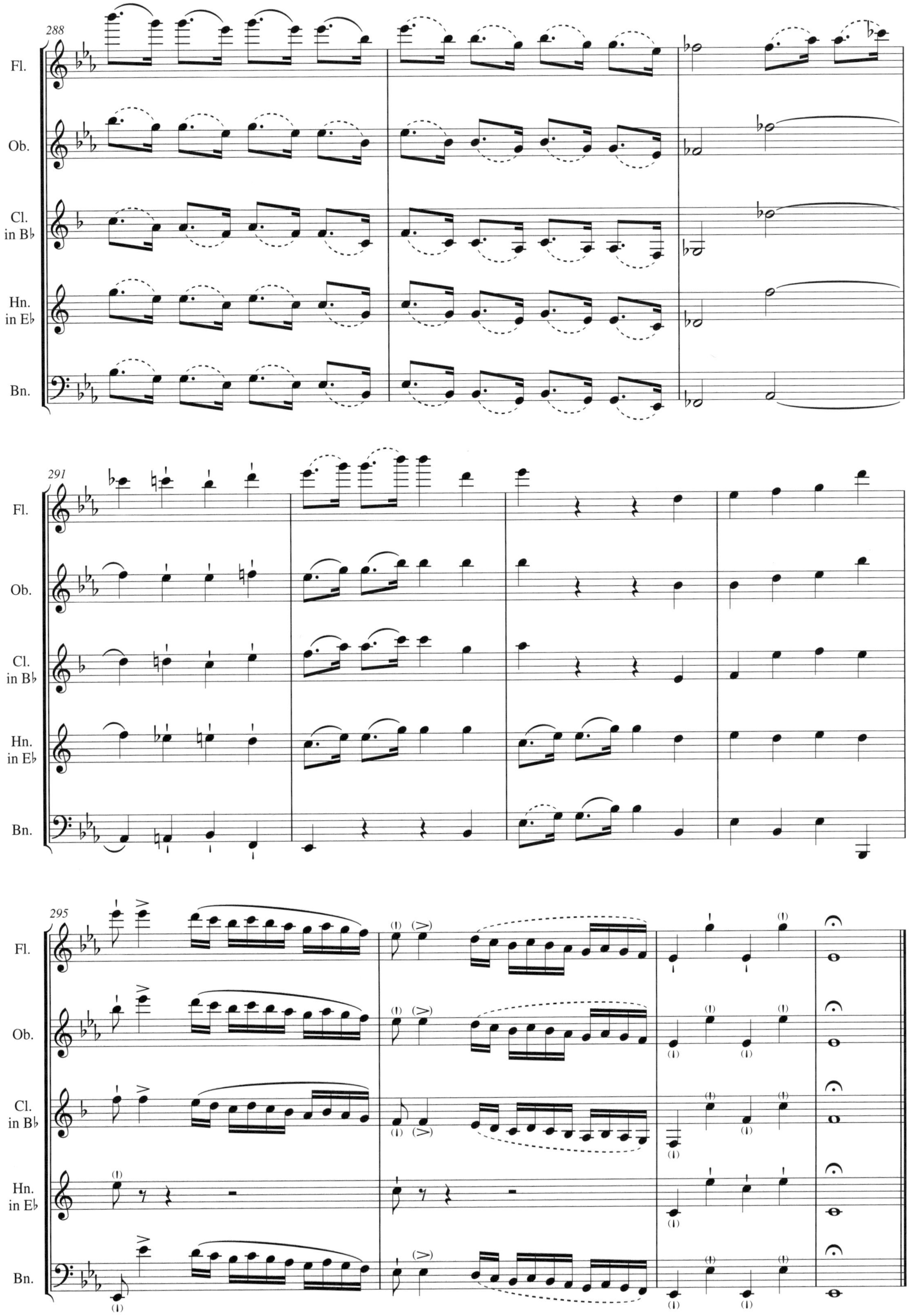
288
Fl.
Ob.
Cl. in B♭
Hn. in E♭
Bn.
291
295

[II]

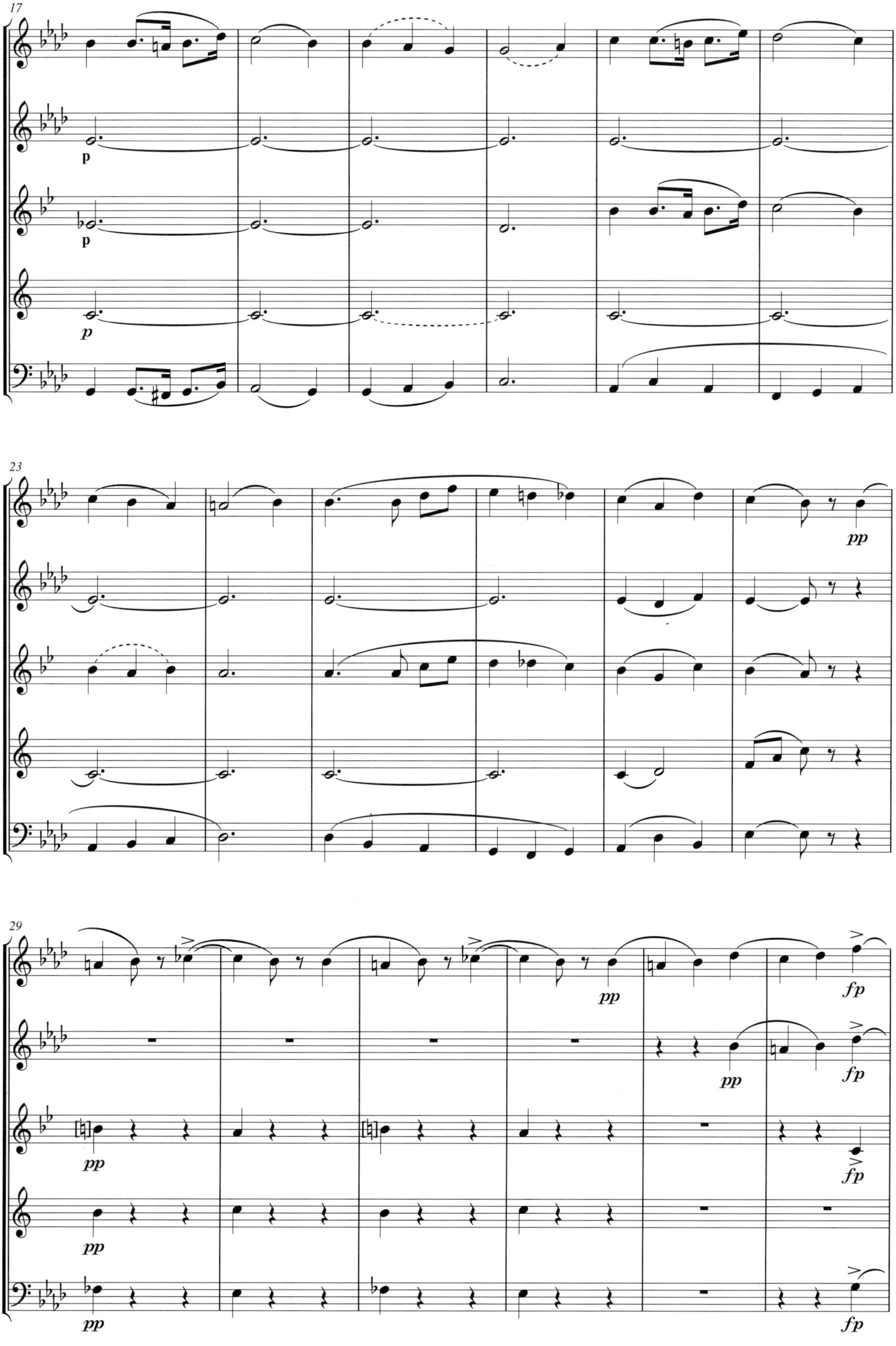
17
Fl.
Ob.
Cl. in B♭
Hn. in E♭
Bn.
p
23
pp
29
fp

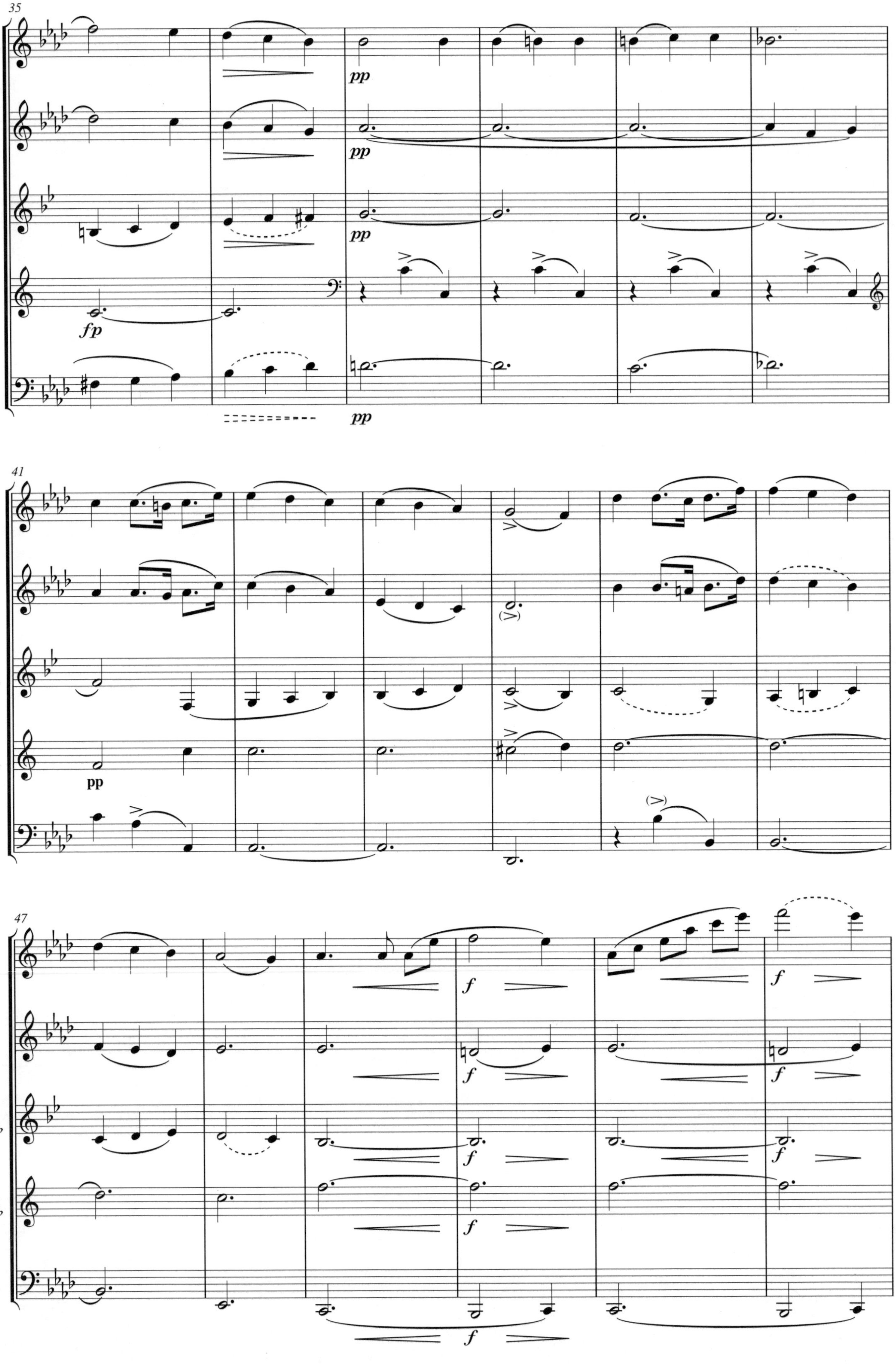
35
Fl.
Ob.
Cl. in B♭
Hn. in E♭
Bn.
pp
fp
41
pp
(>)
47
f

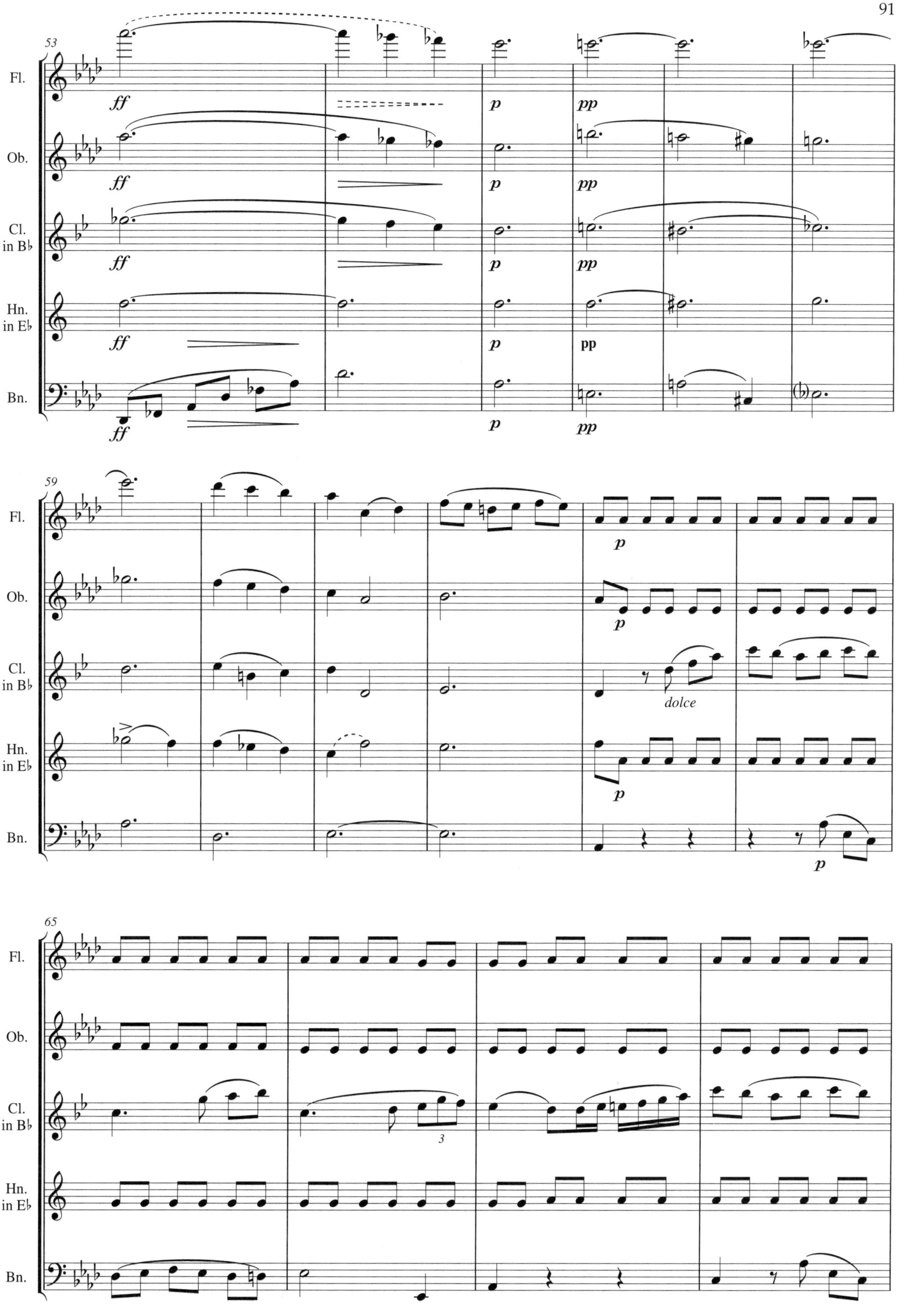
53
Fl.
Ob.
Cl. in B♭
Hn. in E♭
Bn.
ff
p
pp
59
dolce
65
3

69
Fl.
Ob.
Cl. in B♭
Hn. in E♭
Bn.
mf
f
mf
mf
74
pp
pp
pp
pp
pp
p
fp
fp
79
[cresc.]
cresc.
cresc.
cresc.
[cresc.]
fp

93

98
Fl.
Ob.
Cl. in B♭
Hn. in E♭
Bn.
103
Fl.
Ob.
Cl. in B♭
Hn. in E♭
Bn.
108
Fl.
Ob.
Cl. in B♭
Hn. in E♭
Bn.
f
f
f
f
f
(!)
(!)
p

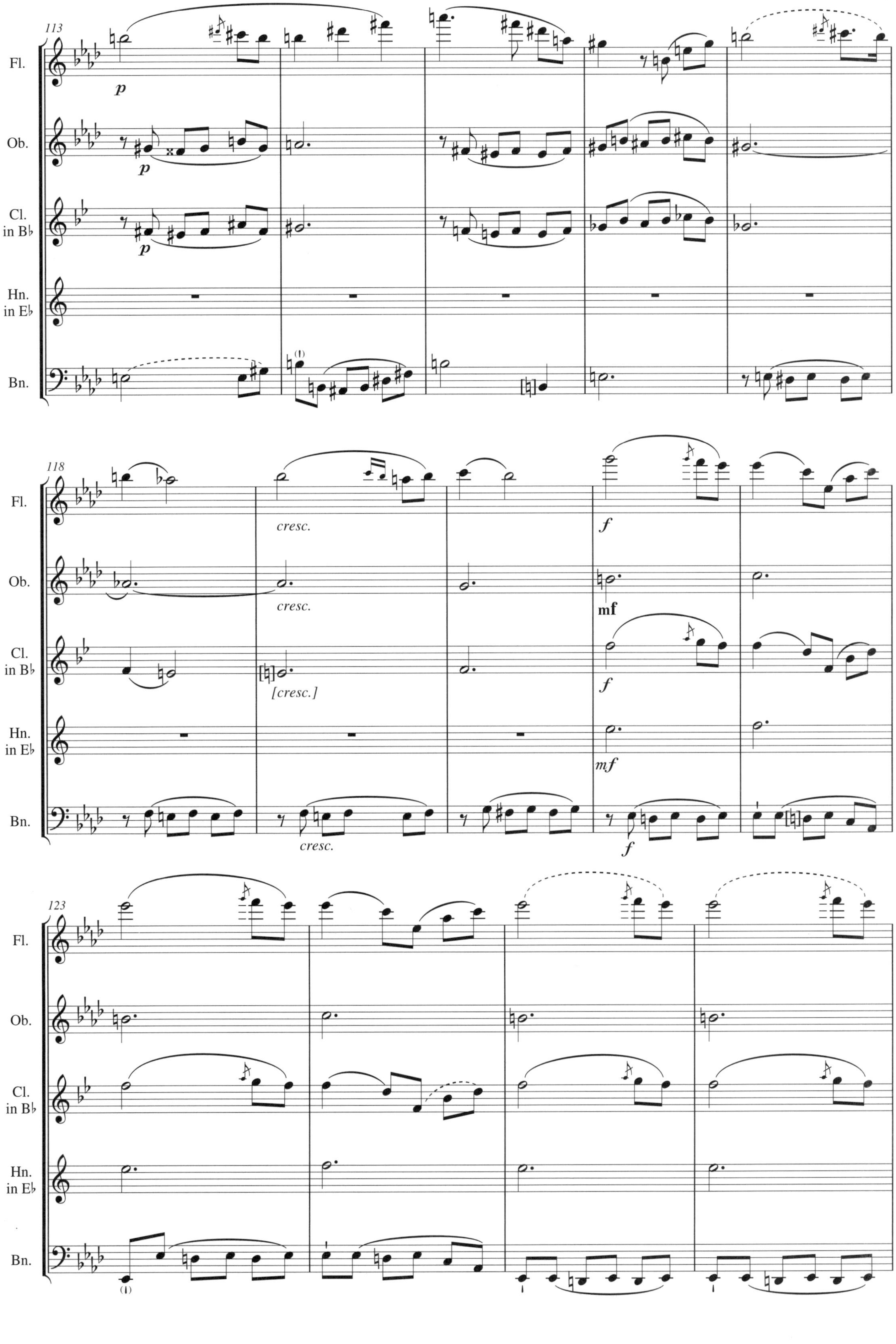
113
Fl.
Ob.
Cl. in B♭
Hn. in E♭
Bn.
p
118
cresc.
[cresc.]
f
mf
123

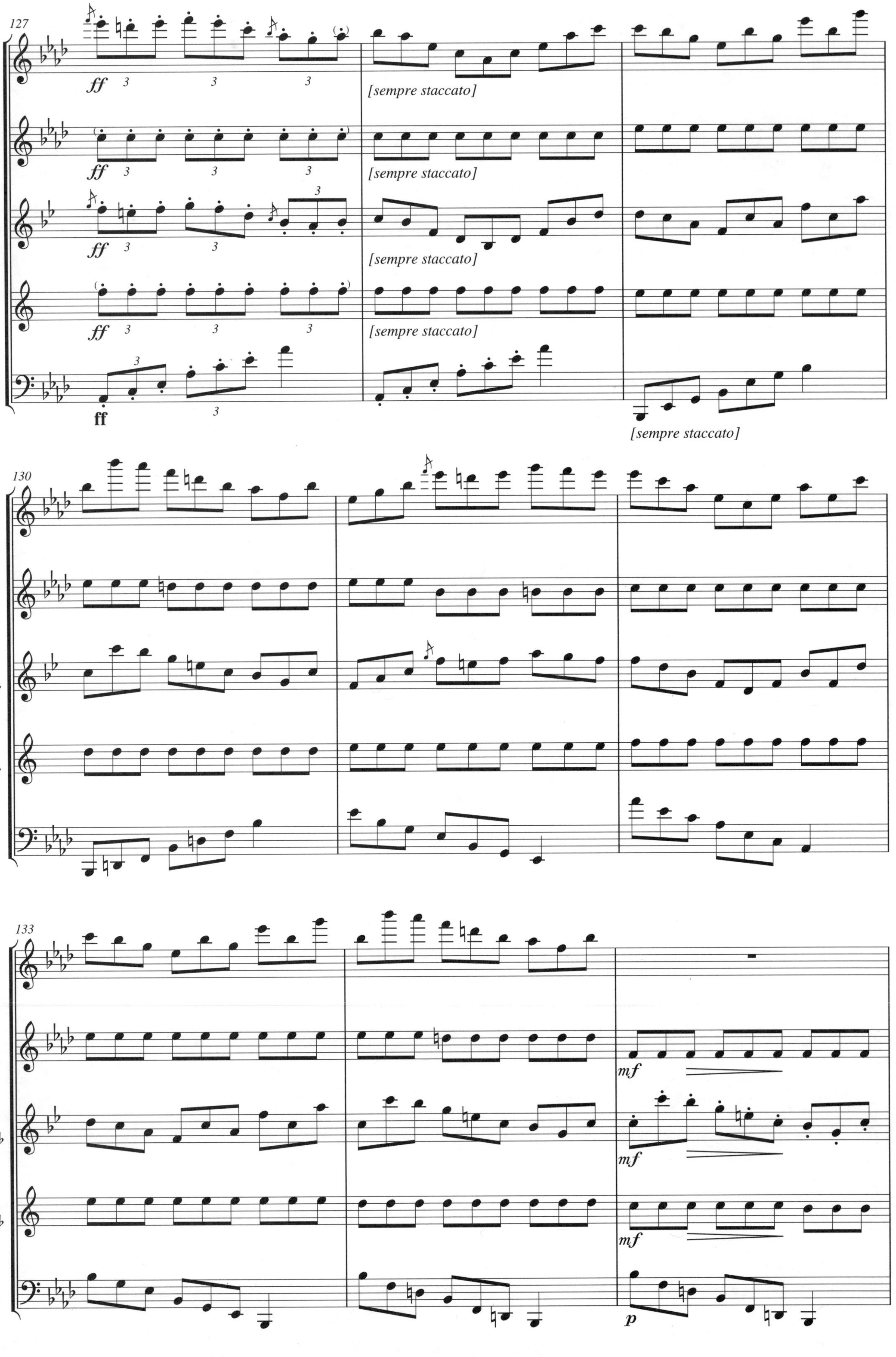
127
Fl.
Ob.
Cl. in B♭
Hn. in E♭
Bn.
ff
[sempre staccato]
130
133
mf
p

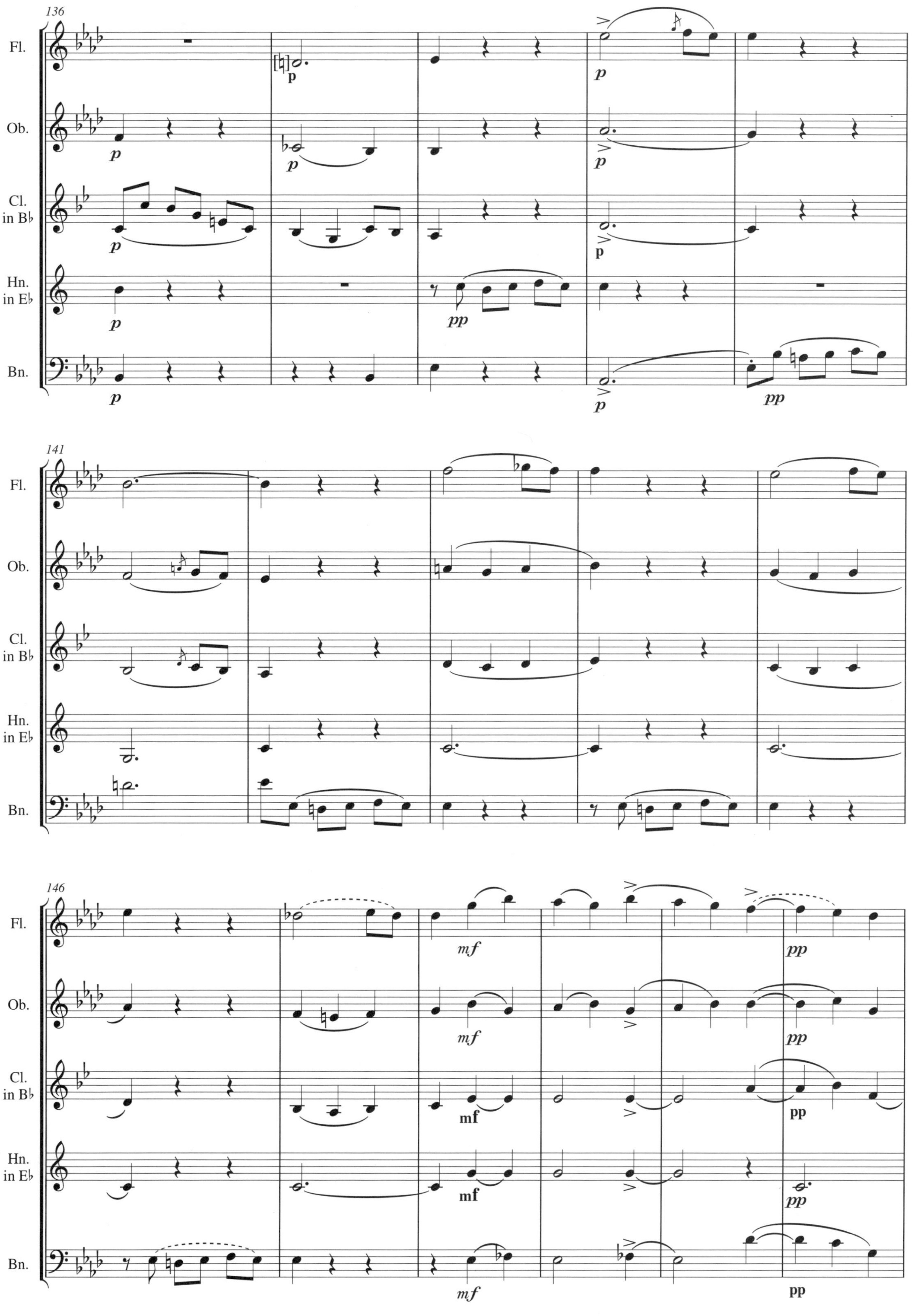
136
Fl.
Ob.
Cl. in B♭
Hn. in E♭
Bn.
p
pp
141
146
mf
pp

152
Fl.
Ob.
Cl. in B♭
Hn. in E♭
Bn.
157
Fl.
Ob.
Cl. in B♭
Hn. in E♭
Bn.
f
f
f
f
f
163
Fl.
Ob.
Cl. in B♭
Hn. in E♭
Bn.
f
f
ff
ff
ff
ff
ff
p
p
p
p
p
pp
pp
pp
pp
pp

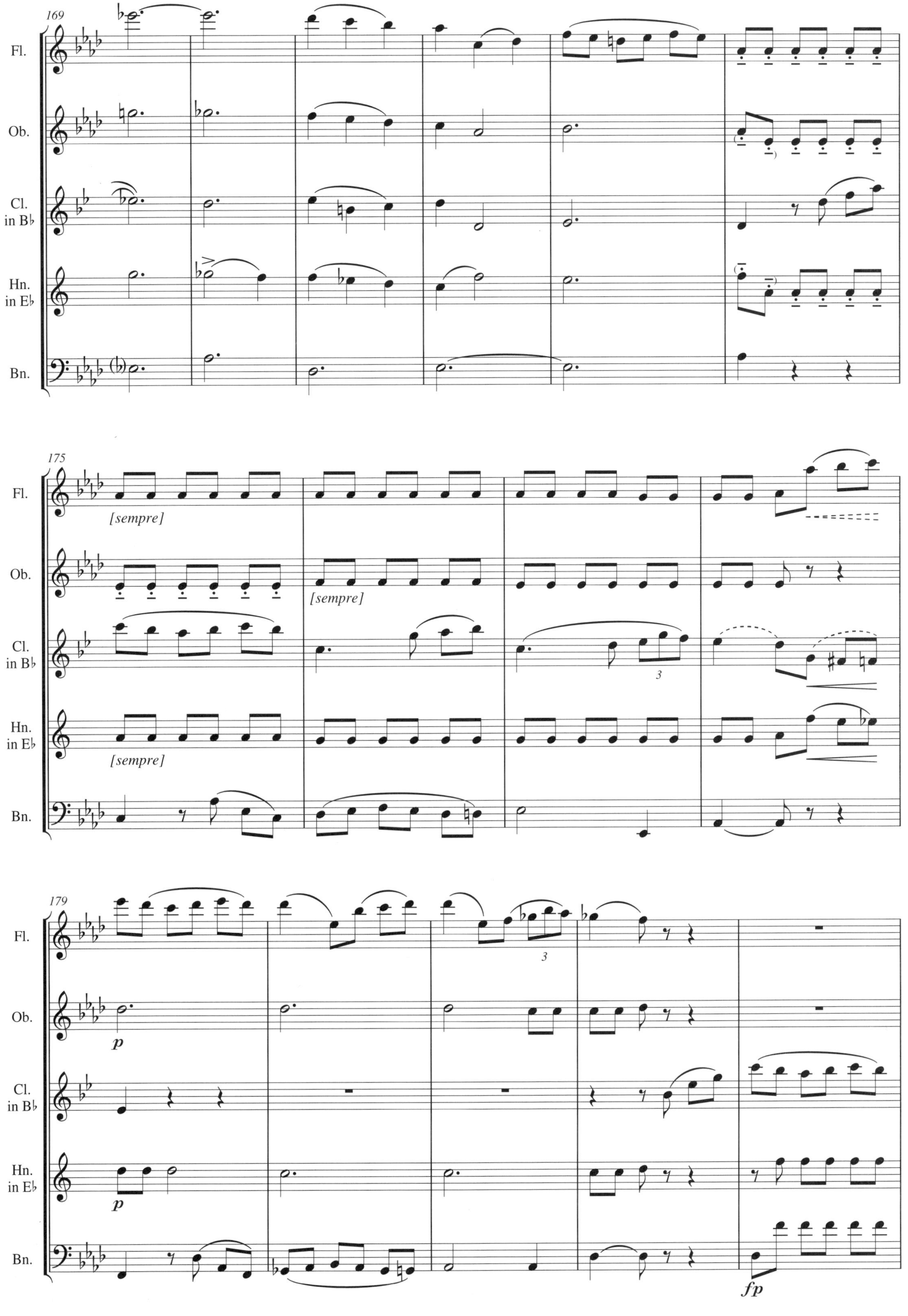
169
Fl.
Ob.
Cl. in B♭
Hn. in E♭
Bn.
175
[sempre]
[sempre]
[sempre]
3
179
p
p
3
fp

184
Fl.
Ob.
Cl. in B♭
Hn. in E♭
Bn.
cresc.
cresc.
cresc.
tr
189
f
p dolce
f
p
f
p
f
f
p
194

101

102

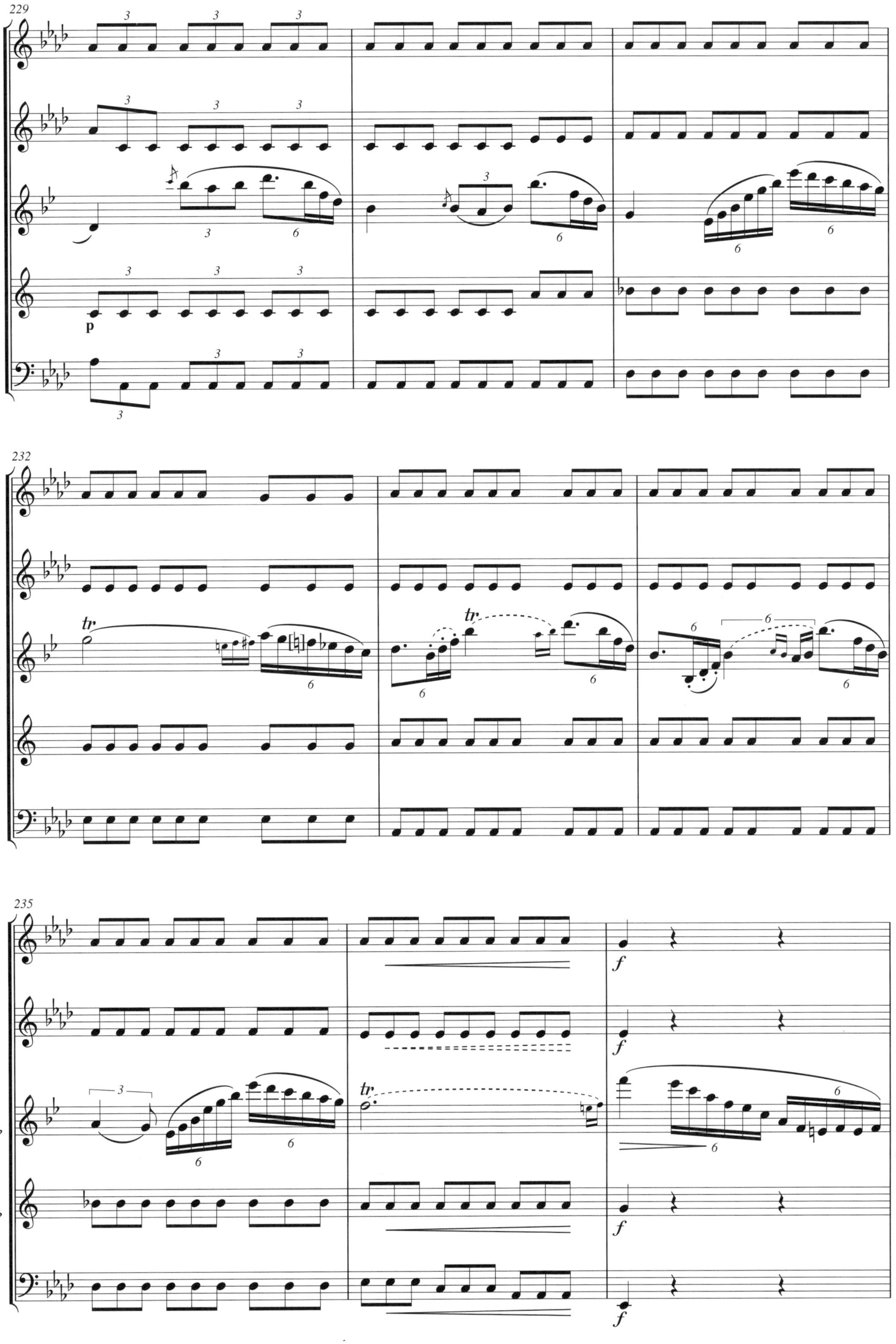
229
Fl.
Ob.
Cl. in B♭
Hn. in E♭
Bn.
232
235

104

105

[III]

Menuetto: Allegro assai

107

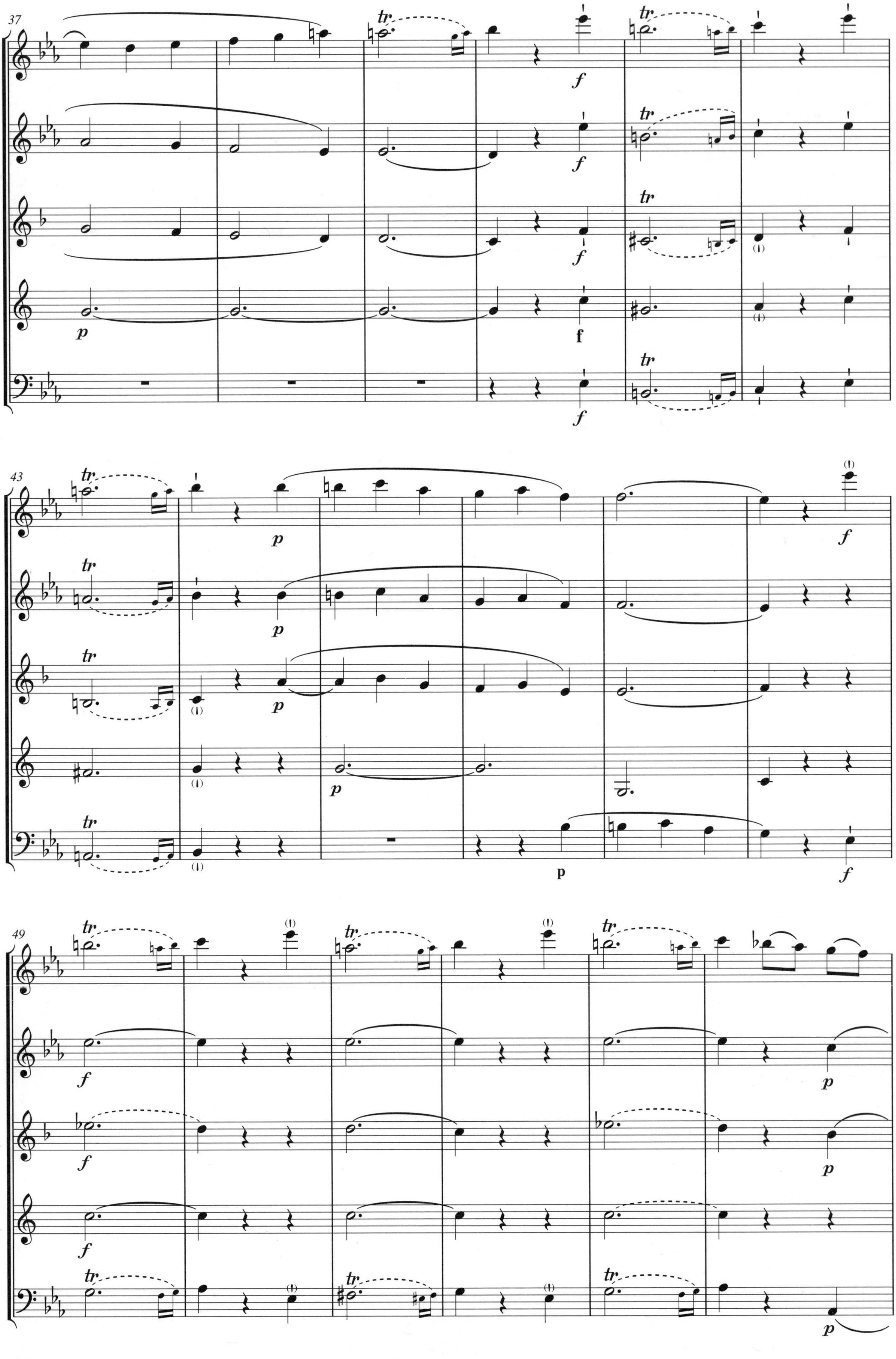
37
Fl.
Ob.
Cl. in B♭
Hn. in E♭
Bn.
tr
f
p
43
49

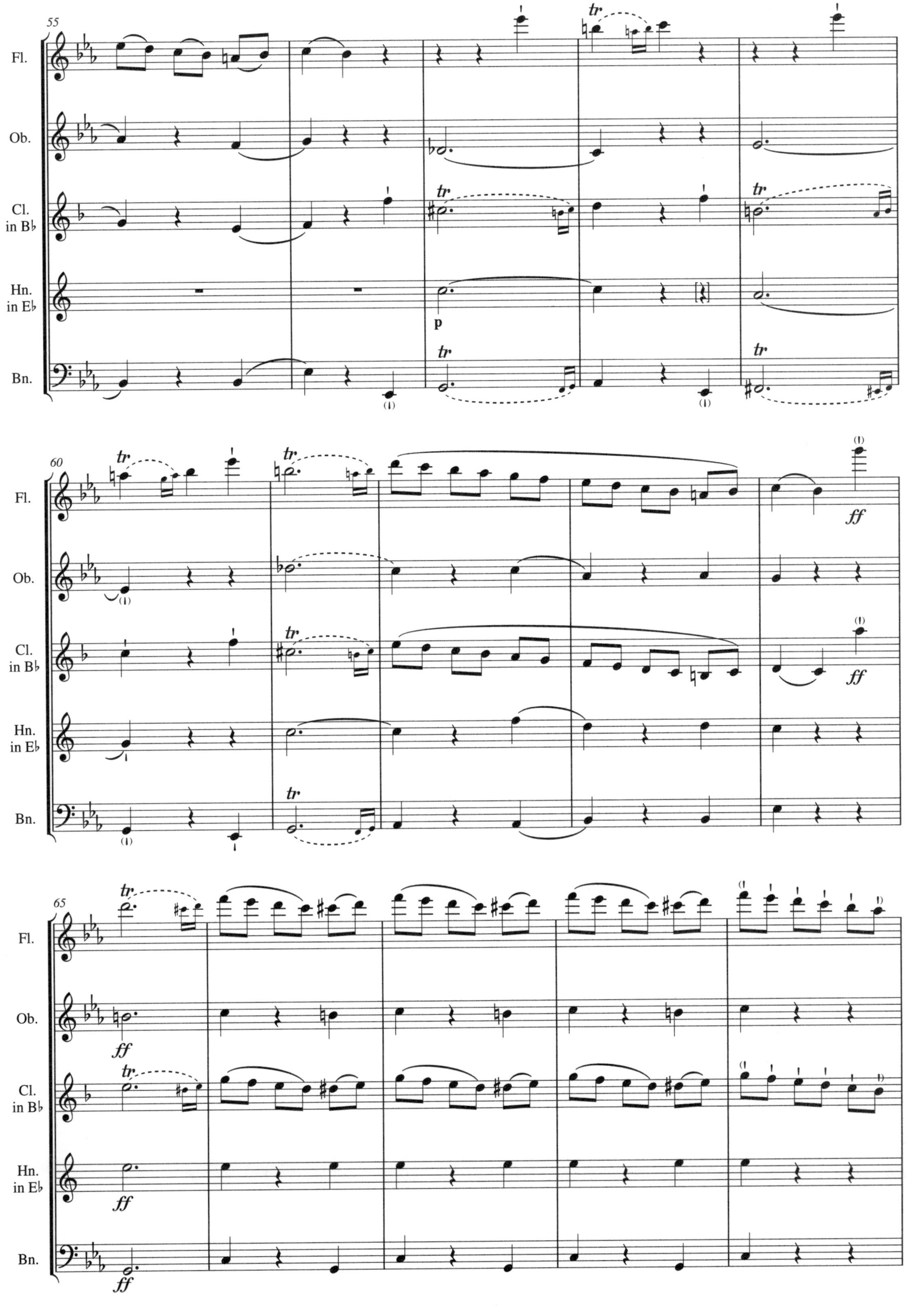
55
Fl.
Ob.
Cl. in B♭
Hn. in E♭
Bn.
tr
p
60
ff
65

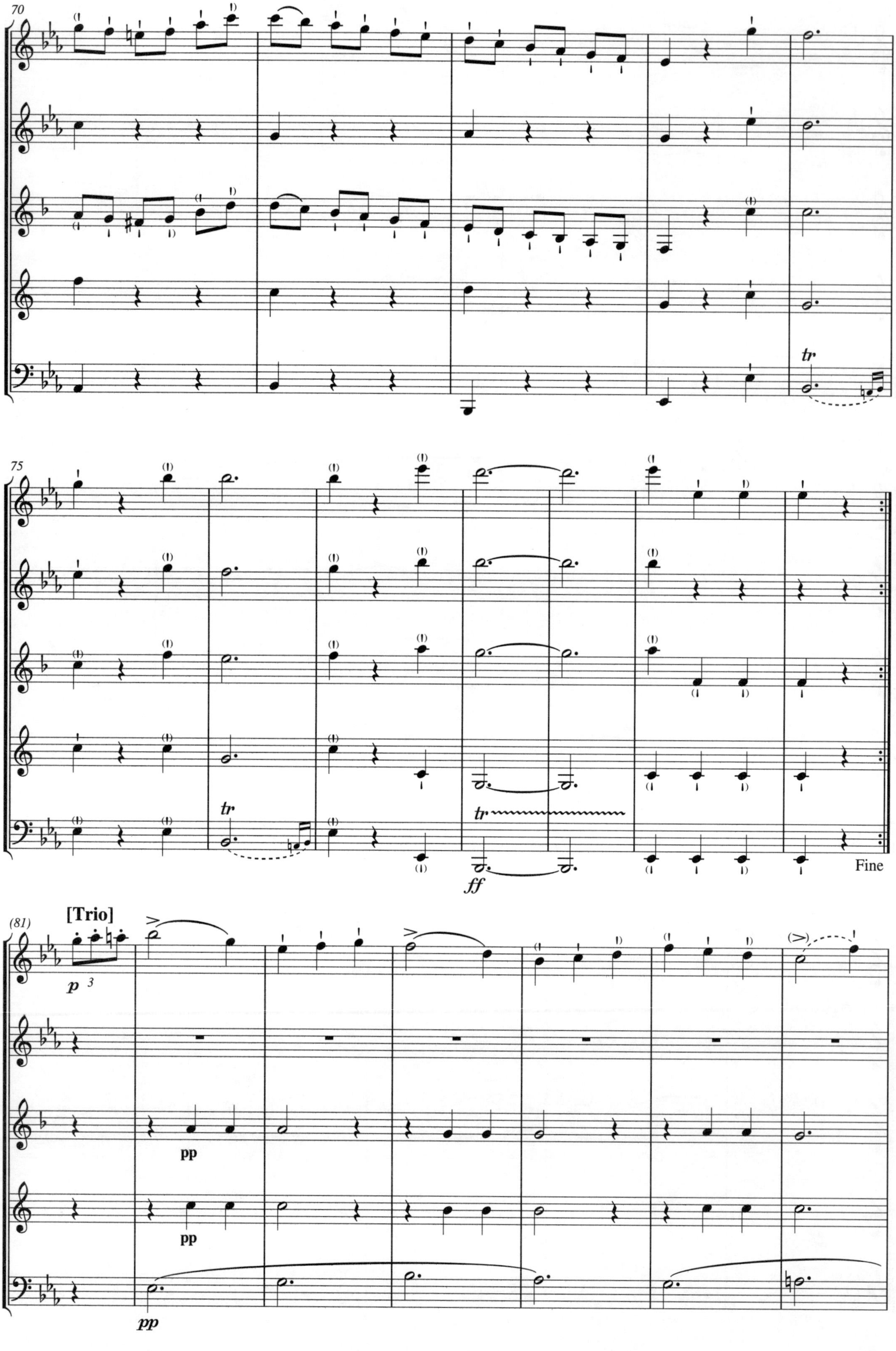
70
Fl.
Ob.
Cl. in B♭
Hn. in E♭
Bn.
tr
75
tr
ff
Fine
(81)
[Trio]
p
pp
pp
pp

111

112

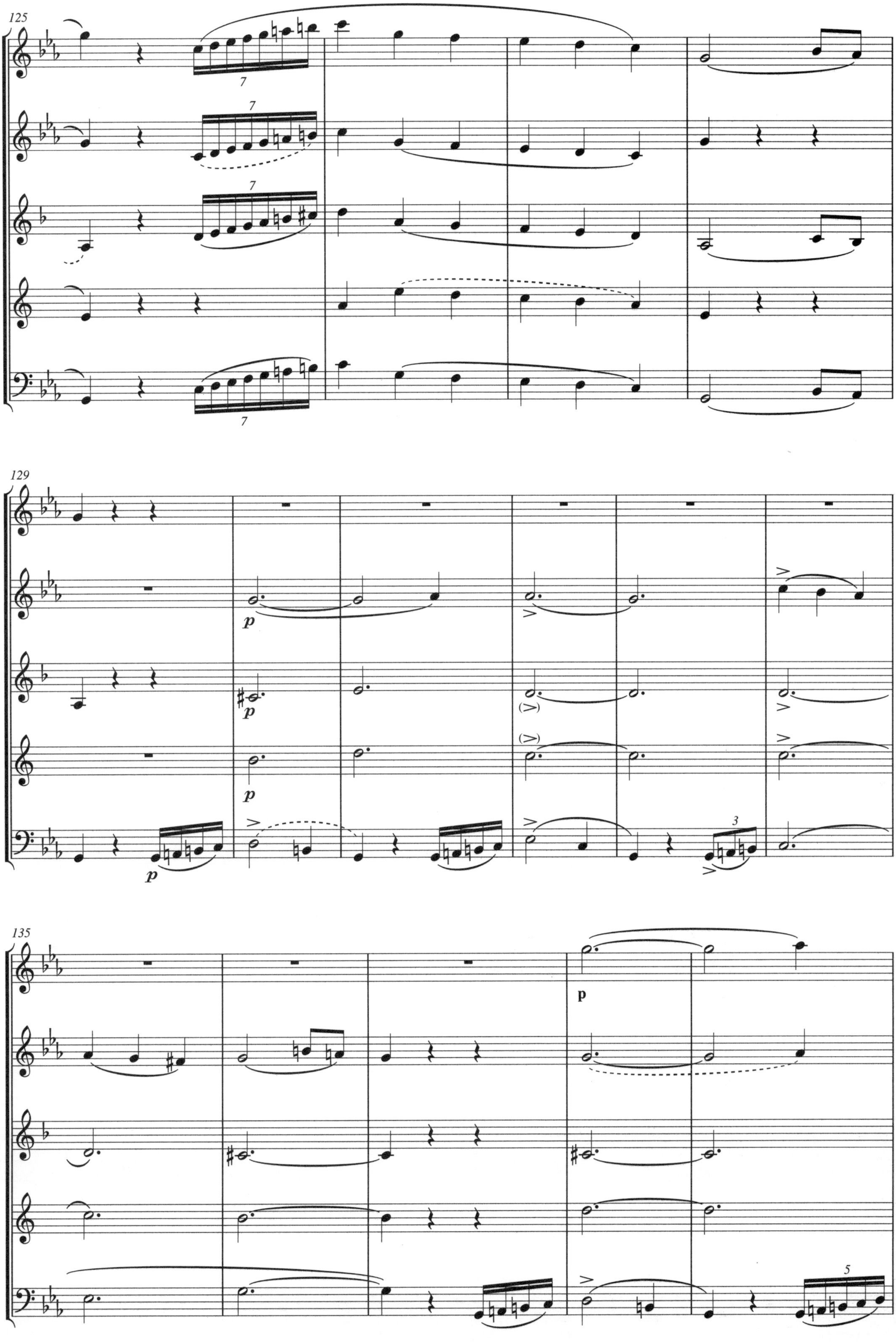
125
Fl.
Ob.
Cl. in B♭
Hn. in E♭
Bn.
7
129
p
(>)
3
135
p
5

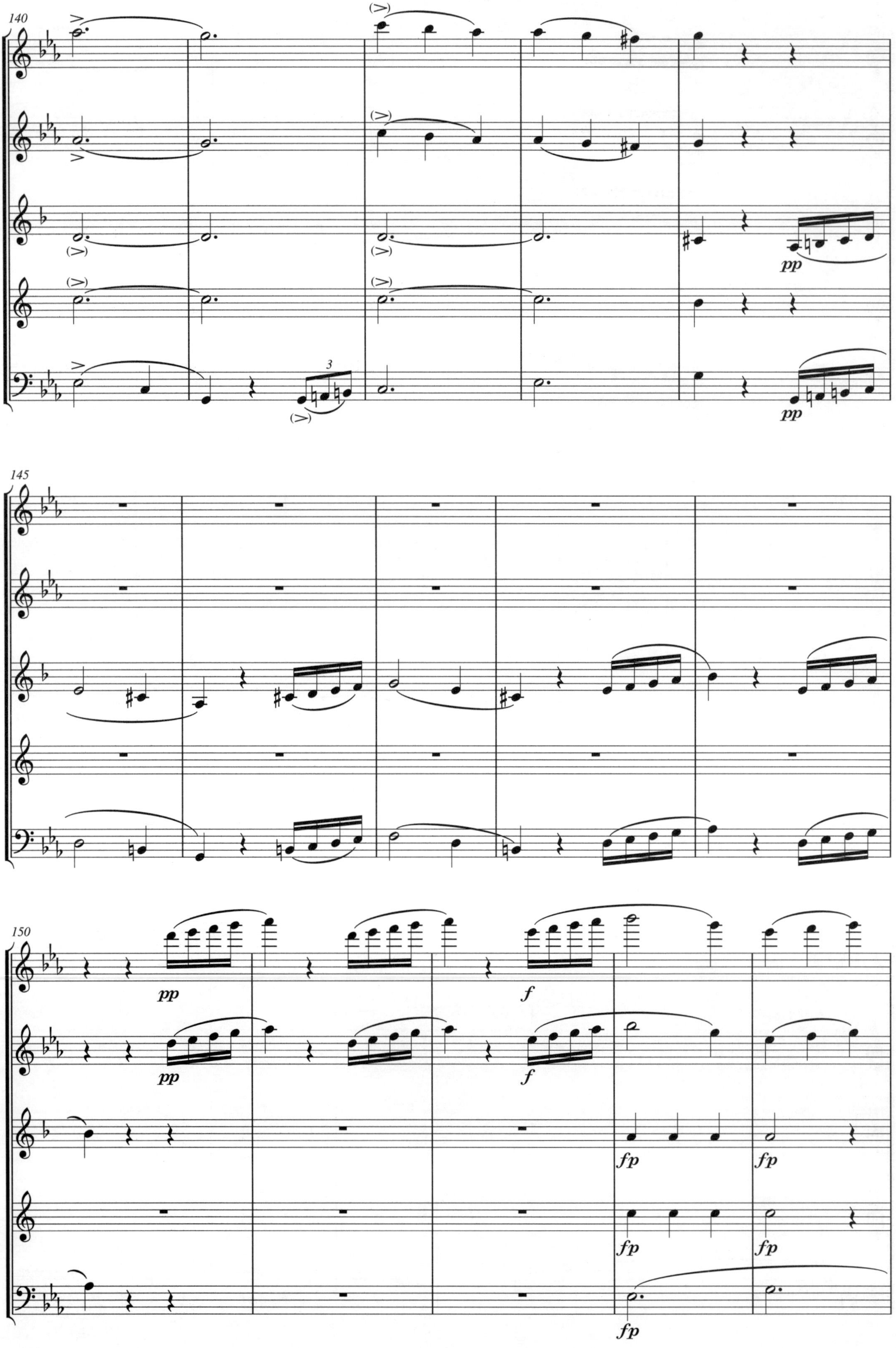
140
Fl.
Ob.
Cl. in B♭
Hn. in E♭
Bn.
(>)
3
pp
145
150
f
fp

Menuetto da capo al fine

[IV]

117

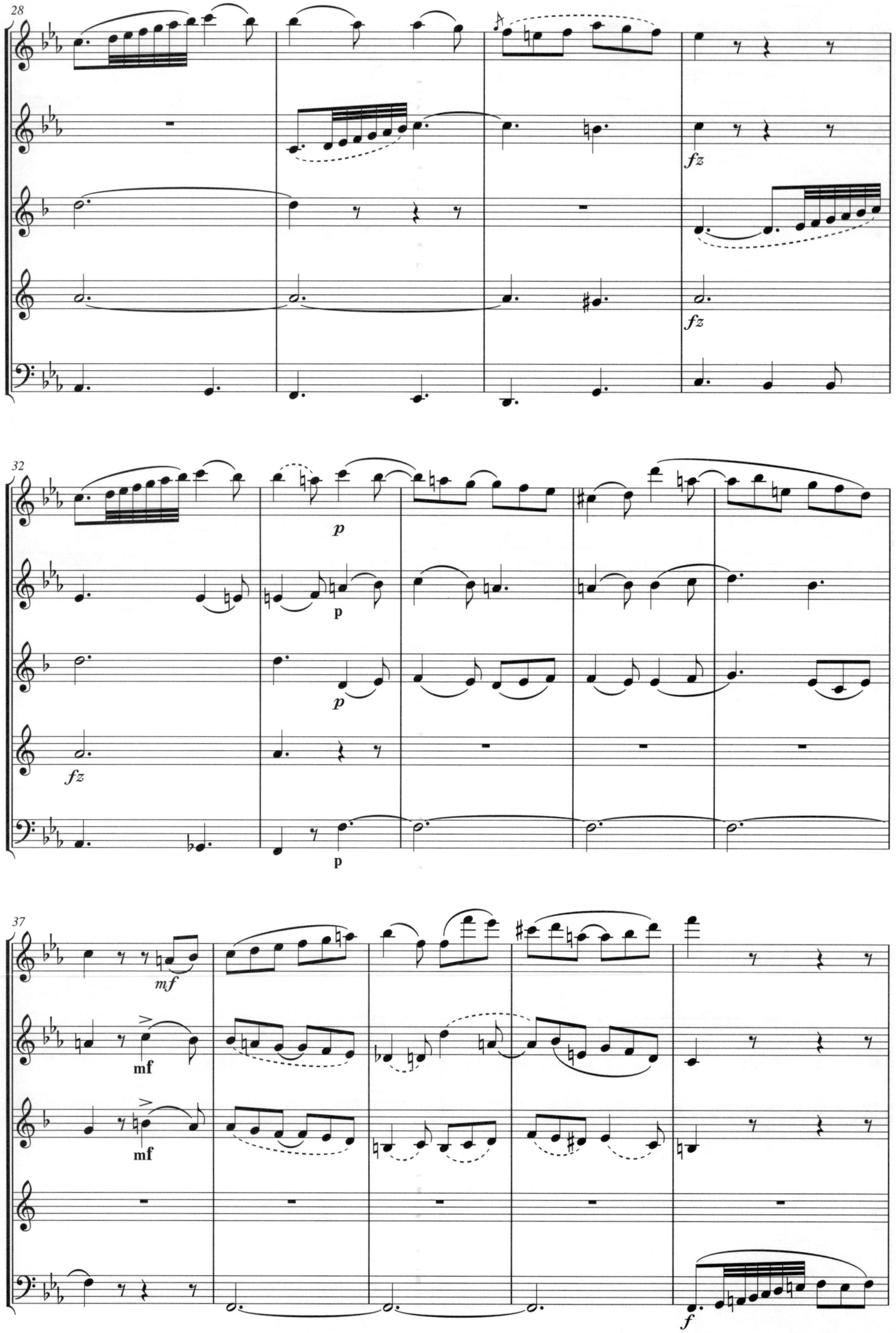
28
Fl.
Ob.
Cl. in B♭
Hn. in E♭
Bn.
fz
fz
32
p
p
p
fz
p
37
mf
mf
mf
f

42
Fl.
Ob.
Cl. in B♭
Hn. in E♭
Bn.
dim.
dim.
dim.
[dim.]
47
p
p con espress.
p
fp
p
52

120

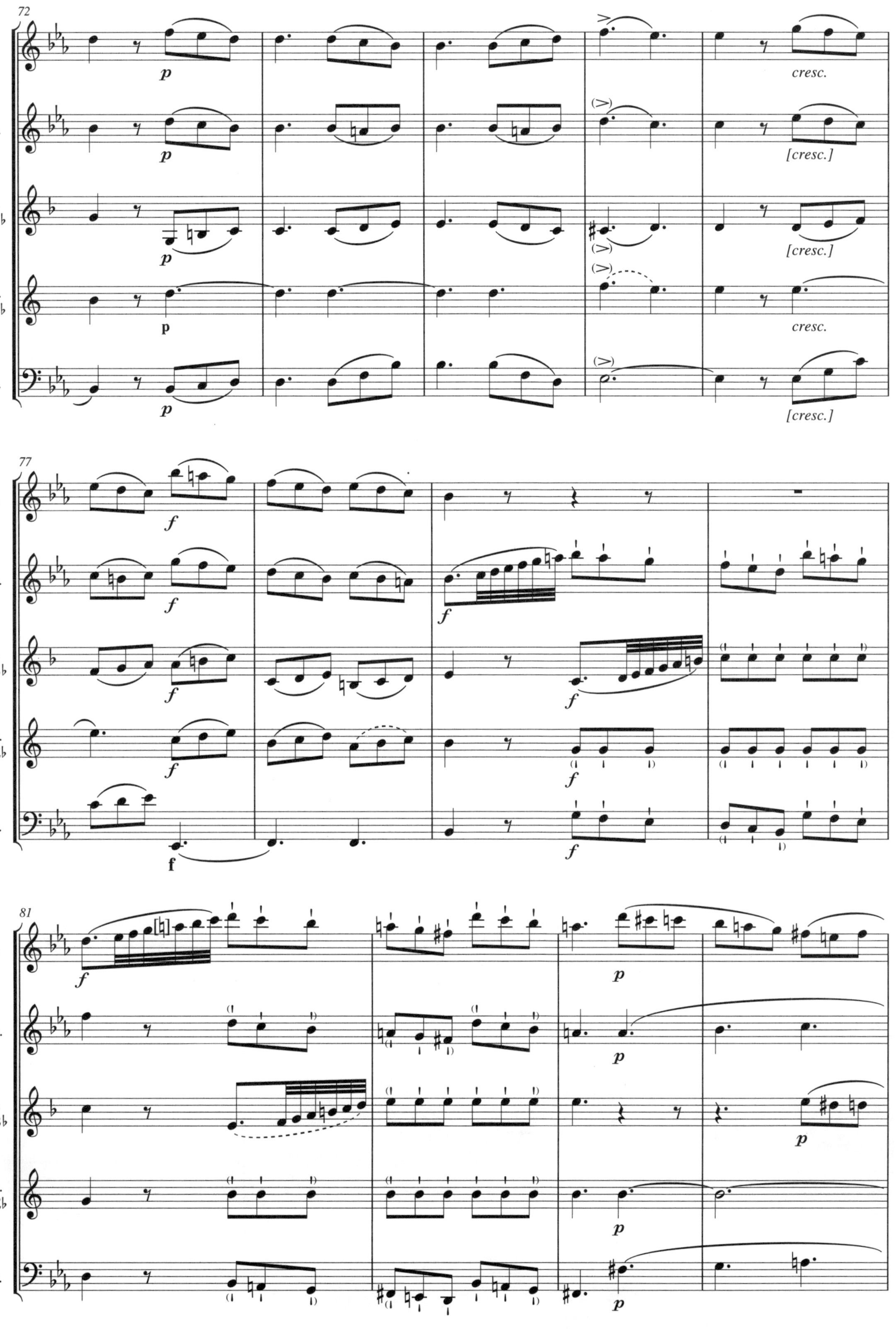
72
Fl.
Ob.
Cl. in B♭
Hn. in E♭
Bn.
p
cresc.
[cresc.]
77
f
81

85
Fl.
Ob.
Cl. in B♭
Hn. in E♭
Bn.
cresc.
cresc.
f
f
f
f
f
90
p
cresc.
p
cresc.
p
[cresc.]
p
cresc.
p
[cresc.]
94

123

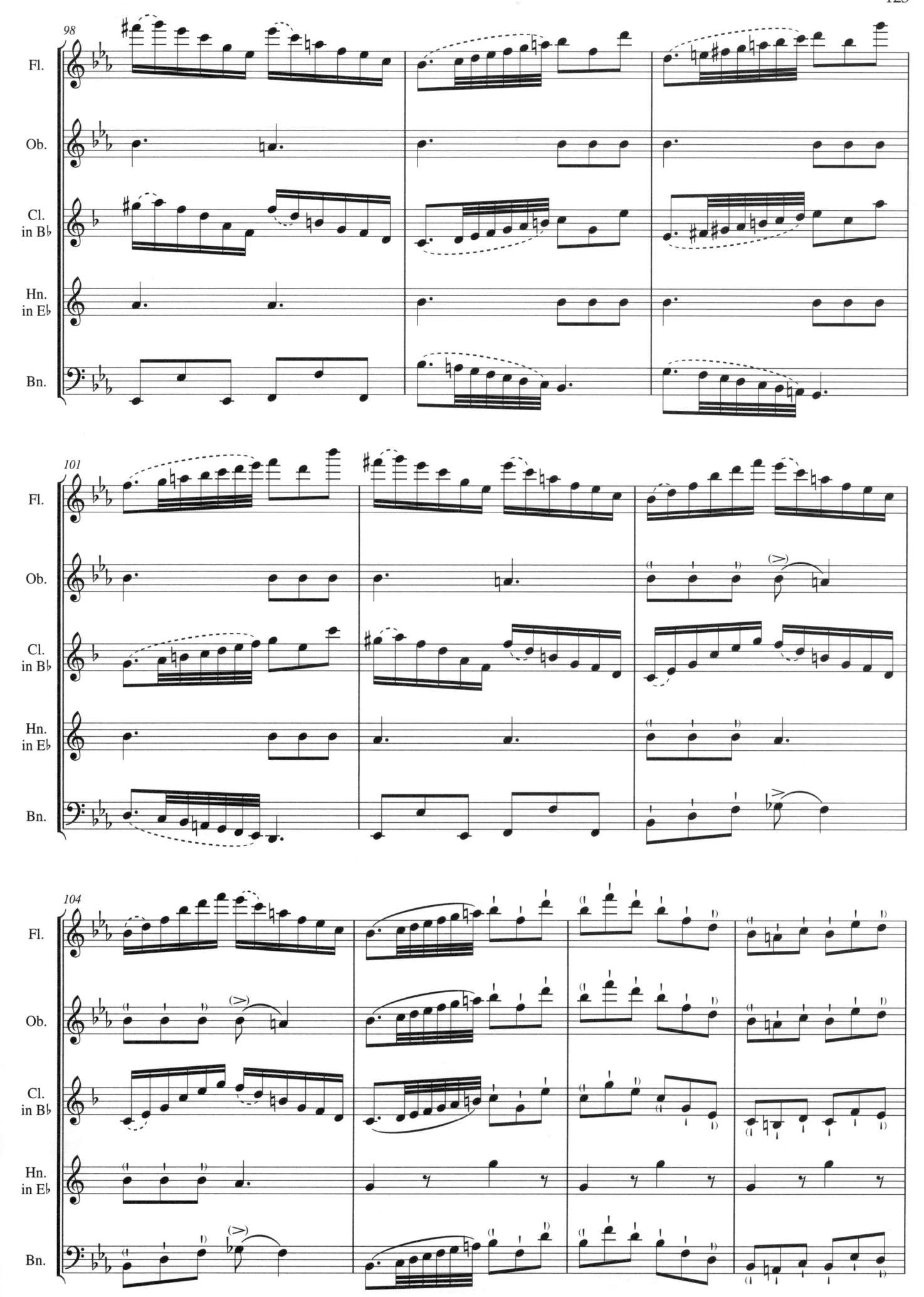

124

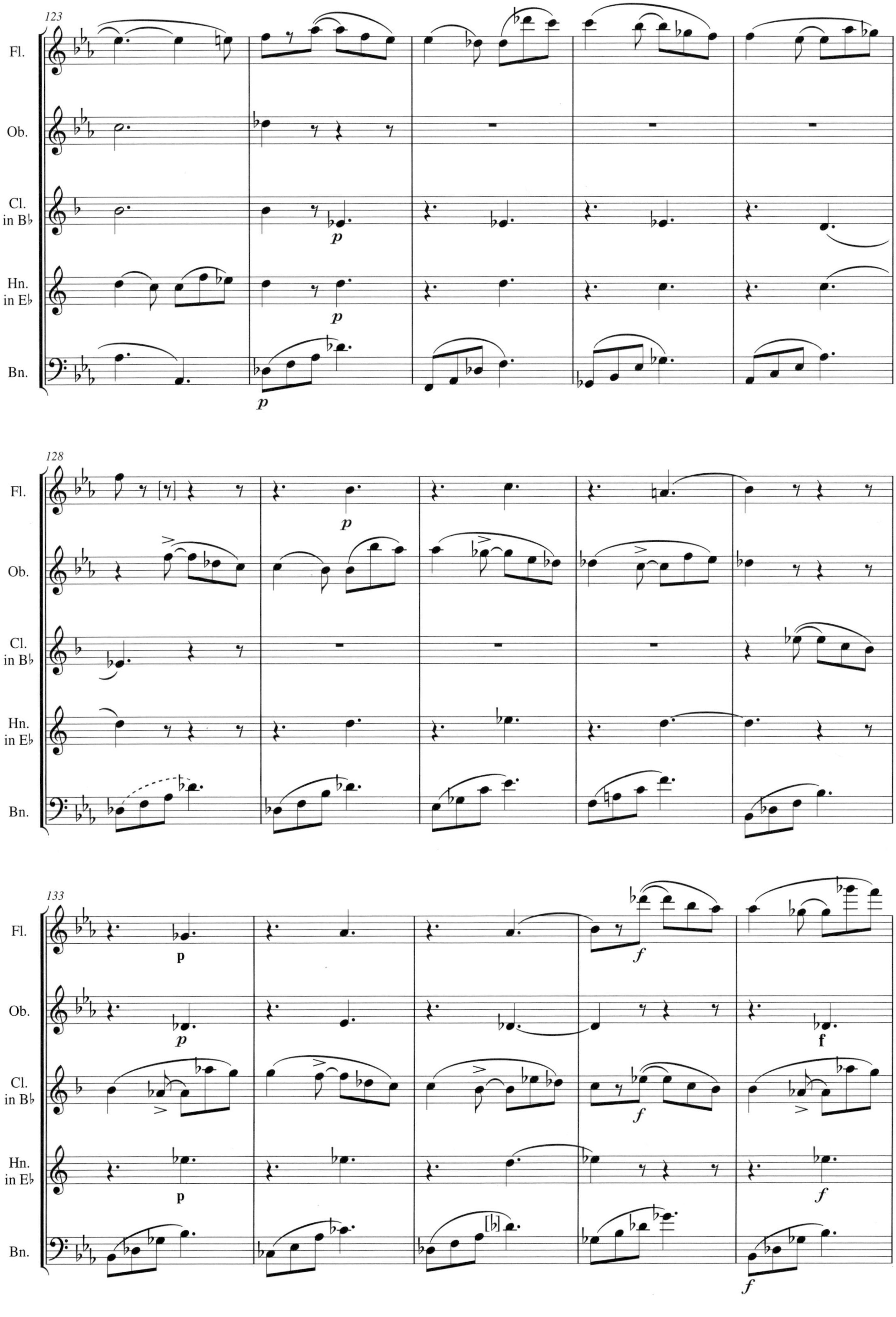
123
Fl.
Ob.
Cl. in B♭
Hn. in E♭
Bn.
128
133

138
Fl.
Ob.
Cl. in B♭
Hn. in E♭
Bn.
p [sempre staccato]
p [sempre staccato]
p [sempre staccato]
143
148
f
f
f
f

153
Fl.
Ob.
Cl. in B♭
Hn. in E♭
Bn.
158
Fl.
Ob.
Cl. in B♭
Hn. in E♭
Bn.
163
Fl.
Ob.
Cl. in B♭
Hn. in E♭
Bn.

128

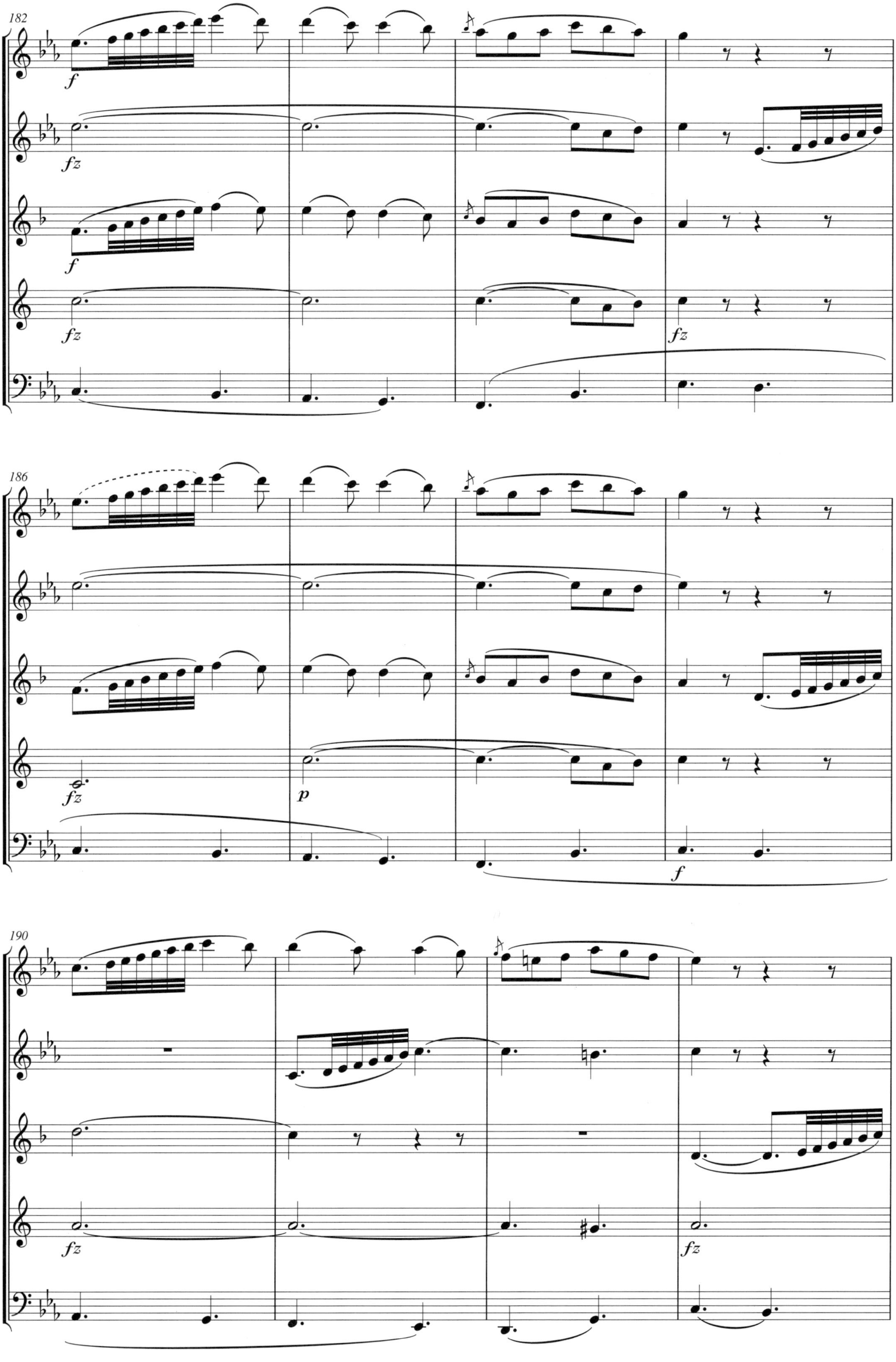
182
186
190
Fl.
Ob.
Cl. in B♭
Hn. in E♭
Bn.
f
fz
p

194
Fl.
Ob.
Cl. in B♭
Hn. in E♭
Bn.
fz
fz
198
Fl.
Ob.
Cl. in B♭
Hn. in E♭
Bn.
fz
fz
202
Fl.
Ob.
Cl. in B♭
Hn. in E♭
Bn.
fz
fz
p
p
p
p

131

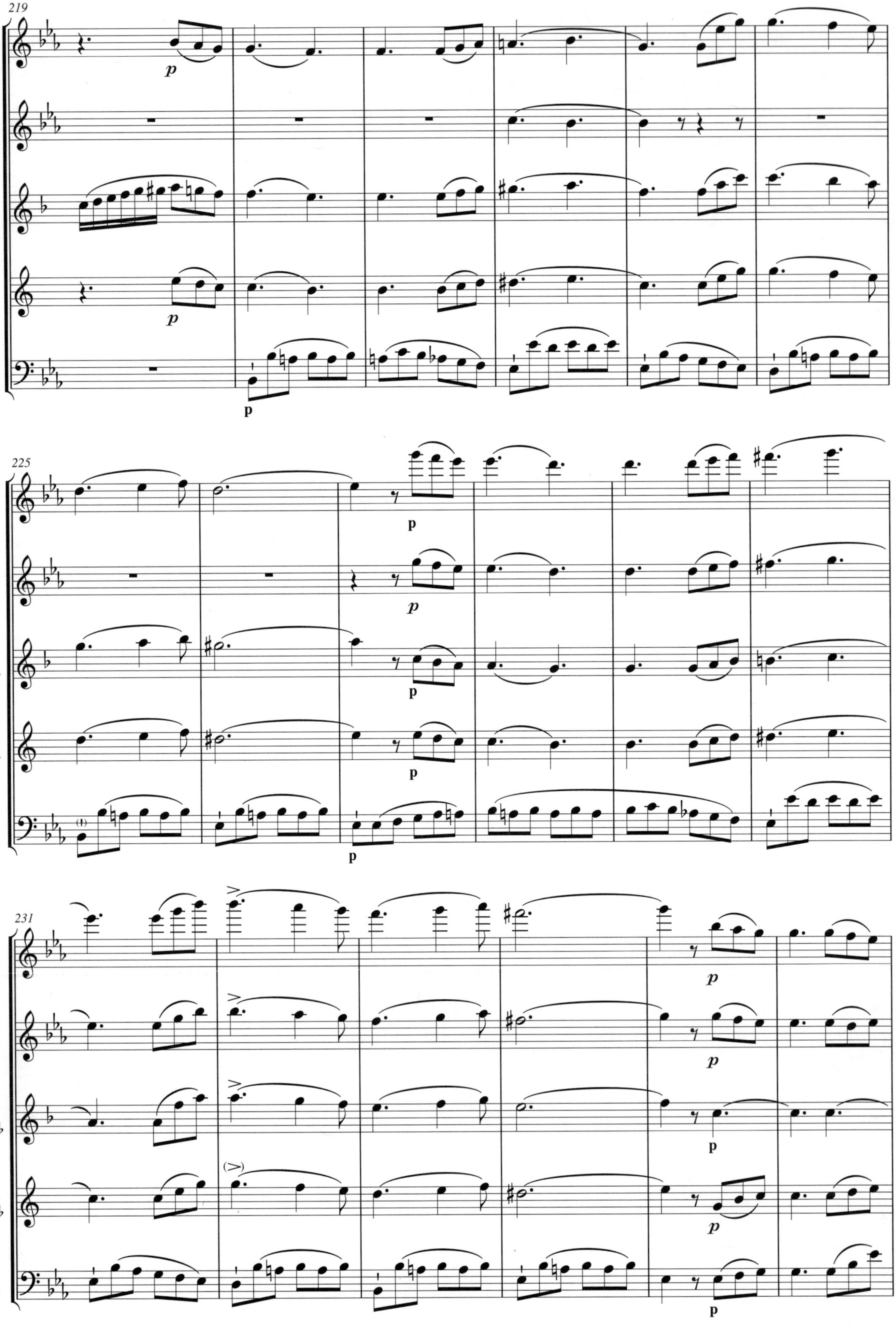
219
Fl.
Ob.
Cl. in B♭
Hn. in E♭
Bn.
p
225
231

133

134

268
Fl.
Ob.
Cl. in B♭
Hn. in E♭
Bn.
fp
p
274
p [sempre staccato]
p [sempre staccato]
279
cresc.
fp

136

299
Fl.
Ob.
Cl. in B♭
Hn. in E♭
Bn.
303
Fl.
Ob.
Cl. in B♭
Hn. in E♭
Bn.
307
Fl.
Ob.
Cl. in B♭
Hn. in E♭
Bn.
p
ff

Critical Report

Sources

The only known sources of the Lachner quintets are the autograph manuscripts currently housed in the Bayerische Staatsbibliothek, Munich (Mus. Mss. 5796 and 5783). These two manuscripts, each containing one quintet, make up the complete woodwind quintet output of the composer. The quintet in F major dates from 1824 while the one in E-flat major dates from 1827.

Woodwind Quintet No. 1 in F Major

The title page reads:

> Quintuor | pour | Flûte, Hautbois, Clarinette, Cor | et Basson | composé | par | François Lachner

On the bottom right of the title page is inscribed "Wien 1824"; slightly above and to the far left of this date, what appears to be the inscription "Oct 29" is found. The page also contains the annotations "Mus. Mss. 5796" and "IV, 8" at the top. The size of the manuscript is approximately 24.5 cm × 30 cm, generally with sixteen staves per page (but see below). The manuscript has frayed edges but is in reasonably good condition. The library name is stamped at the very bottom of the title page.

There are two versions of movements 1 and 2 included in the manuscript. The critical notes below refer to the newer/revised versions unless otherwise noted. The older versions have sixteen staves per page, typically starting on the top staff and running three systems with an extra staff at the bottom only; the newer versions have eighteen staves per page, typically starting on the top staff and running three systems with an open staff under each. The revised versions are in front and constitute a cleaner, newer copy; the older versions follow and begin the pagination over again.

Woodwind Quintet No. 2 in E-flat Major

The title page reads:

> Quintett für Blasinstrumente | Nr. 2 Es-Dur

The indication "Nr. 2 Es-Dur" is written in a different hand than the main title; this is also the case for the inscription of the date, "1827," on the upper right of the page. The title page also contains the annotations "Mus. Mss. 5783" and "IV, 12" at the top. The size of the manuscript is approximately 24.5 cm × 30 cm, with sixteen staves per page. The edges of the manuscript are frayed but it is in reasonably good condition. Towards the middle-right of the title page, "Lachner" is written in broad strokes, and the library name is stamped at the very bottom.

It is interesting to note that Lachner used a different language for each quintet title page. The use of French for the first quintet reflects the importance of Paris to the early history of wind quintets. Lachner's use of German for his second quintet shows his greater comfort at this point with his native tradition.

While speculative in nature, some thoughts regarding use of staff paper might prove helpful. Since the newer revisions of Quintet No. 1 were done on eighteen-staff paper, while the older versions and Quintet No. 2 were written on sixteen-staff paper, this would seem to imply that Quintet No. 2 might predate the revision done to Quintet No. 1. Given that the works were three years apart, the revision might have come well after the composition. On the other hand, Lachner might simply have used different paper just for the revisions themselves.

Editorial Method

As noted above, this edition is based solely on the autograph manuscripts of the Lachner quintets. The edition makes clear the original notations of the autograph manuscripts and distinguishes these from any editorial additions or clarifications, as follows: most added markings are placed in brackets; added articulations are placed in parentheses; added hairpins, slurs, and ties are dashed; added letter dynamics are set in bold type rather than the customary bold-italic; any other deviation from the originals are listed in the critical notes.

The instrument names and abbreviations—written in Italian in the autographs—are given in English. Tempo indications and other performance instructions have been modernized and regularized for orthography and spelling (such as adding the accent in *Più mosso* and changing *cres.* to *cresc.*). Barlines are modernized but sectional thin-thin barlines have been retained. Rest patterns are regularized and modernized (as in using a dotted quarter rest for the first half of a $^6_8$ measure). Beamings are modernized. The indications of triplets and other groupettes are regularized (e.g., once a pattern is established, subsequent indications are removed). The modern method of notating the horn part higher than sounding pitch in passages in bass clef—as in the treble clef—is utilized (whereas Lachner notated the part lower in bass clef).

The editorial approach used will be further summarized through the following discussion of nine broad topics: articulations, dynamic markings, erasures, pitches and accidentals, trills and grace notes, shortcuts, rhythmic issues, corollary material, and conflicting material.

Articulations

One of the most difficult issues in editing the quintets dealt with questions regarding articulations. This broad topic will be divided into two categories in order to best illustrate the decisions involved.

PLACEMENT OF SLURS

Lachner uses slurs frequently throughout both quintets, although their placement can be at times ambiguous. Ambiguity results primarily from inconsistent or careless application. Some slurs are so long that they seem to be denoting phrases more than indicating specific slur patterns.

In the autograph manuscripts, Lachner tends to draw slurs and ties one after the other, so that one tie or slur ends on the same note where a new slur begins. There are cases, however, where ties are enclosed by slurs in the sources, and these have been reflected literally in all such cases within the edition. With regard to slurs directly following slurs, these have been combined into single slurs in the edition with critical notes added to report the adjustments.

Despite the need to combine some slurs, all slurs indicated in the autographs have been replicated in this edition as close as possible to their original intent. For example, in the first movement of Quintet No. 2, measure 117 in the autograph is ambiguous with regard to the flute and horn slurs—the flute slur starts on beat 2 while the horn slur starts in between beats 1 and 2. This passage is echoed immediately, however, and measure 119 in the autograph clearly slurs all four beats together in both parts. In this case, since the first passage is ambiguous and the second unequivocal, both passages were given the four-beat slurring pattern. The opening octave motive of the same movement is found both in slurred and non-slurred forms. The initial statement is slurred in all instruments (m. 1), but see measures 151–64, which has the motive both slurred and unslurred in various instruments. Dashed slurs are added here and in other, even more obvious cases where slurring was clearly intended but accidentally omitted (e.g., m. 150, oboe part). Slurring techniques in the first movement of Quintet No. 1 are quite subtle: while slurs that lead up to the main motive do not slur over the barline (e.g., mm. 31–32, 37–38, 63–64), other similar passages are meant to press forward and do slur over to the downbeat of the next measure (e.g., mm. 69–71, 71–73). Other discrepancies of slurring due to oversight have been corrected and noted in the critical notes or shown through dashed slurs. The main motive of the first movement of Quintet No. 1, Allegro assai—the gesture ♩ ♫ ♩ —is given a staccato on the last quarter note the first time it appears, but all other times there is no staccato. Due to the consistency of the latter, the distinction has been maintained (see m. 28 versus m. 30).

AMBIGUOUS MARKINGS

There are two basic areas of ambiguous markings in the Lachner quintets. The first involves the notation >, which could be interpreted as either an accent or a brief diminuendo. In most cases, the placement over a note (as opposed to in between notes) seems to clarify the situation, but the length of the mark at times makes it more ambiguous. Measure 133 of the third movement of Quintet No. 2, for example, has an accent marking which takes up almost the whole triplet figure in the bassoon part, but given the context (numerous accent marks in other parts), it seems clear Lachner intends the mark to denote an accent. In measure 42 of the fourth movement of the same quintet, however, a very similar notation as the one described above (this time below the bassoon part) would seem to indicate a diminuendo.

The second area of ambiguous markings, and by far one of the most difficult issues in editing these works, is the distinction between the staccato dot and the staccato stroke. The problem is two-fold: first, there is simply no consistency of application for these notations, so that a given passage will in one instance be so marked, but in another appearance have no indication at all; moreover, not all parts of a passage might be indicated, even though it would seem obvious that all should match articulations. The second problem is the confusion of the marks themselves. Many of the markings could be construed physically as representing either a dot or a brief stroke. No doubt, many of these markings were done quickly and in a casual manner, hence leading to their lack of clarity and spotty nature.

Regarding the consistency of application, some cases are quite clear: measure 205 of the first movement of Quintet No. 2 has the stroke marking for all parts on a descending scale; while measure 206 has no markings in the autograph, it is obvious the continuation of the scalar descent should be articulated in the same fashion. Other cases are more ambiguous: measure 291 of the same movement is marked with strokes, while a similar passage three measures later is not. Where such discrepancies appear to be due to simple oversights, then, articulation markings in parentheses have generally been included as the editor's suggestion, but in order to avoid too many intrusions, some of these spots (like the one just mentioned) have been left reflecting the original, and the performers can decide for themselves.

Another passage marked by the inconsistent application of articulations is in the third movement of Quintet No. 1: the section beginning with measure 53 is clearly marked staccato in all parts, and following this is the single annotation "sempre staccatto" [sic]. Thereafter, staccato markings show up sporadically (shown in this edition), even though the intention is clear that this articulation be used consistently through measure 72 by all parts. The annotation has therefore been added editorially to the oboe, clarinet, horn, and bassoon, with the original given to the flute. A similar situation occurs later in the same movement, in the Allegro section of measures 81–147, where throughout, the application of staccato markings is inconsistent. But here, editorial staccatos have been added where appropriate until measure 132, at which point Lachner truly gives up on marking in staccatos and "sempre staccato" has been added editorially in all the parts. Movement 4 of Quintet No. 2 offers yet another interesting example of inconsistent articulation markings: while the passage beginning at measure 141 has strokes for the flute only, the recurrence of the passage at measure 171 with strokes in all parts except the bassoon would seem to indicate Lachner's ultimate intent, even though the passage distinguishes a "solo" part (flute) and "accompaniment," which could be used to explain the articulation differences. Like the example above, in order to avoid numerous editorial markings, I placed "sempre staccato" indications in the oboe, clarinet, and horn at measure 141.

In preparing the edition, the stroke only seemed applicable in the second quintet, where one also finds clear indications of the staccato dot. In the third movement, for instance, the flute's triplet anacrusis to measure 82—the opening of the trio—is unambiguously marked with staccato dots and is immediately followed by an accented half note. As the following measure features quarter notes with strokes, the passage presents an interesting amalgamation of three major articulation types.

Dynamic Markings

While the actual markings used by Lachner are quite common, their location can make the composer's intent ambiguous; it was therefore necessary to regularize and adjust placements in the edition as called for by the musical context. Hairpin markings are used interchangeably with the notations "cres." and "dim." and all of these, along with a wide range of letter dynamics—from *ppp* to *fff*—can be found above, below, or in between staves in the autographs, making it at times difficult to know which instrument was meant to be affected, or if, indeed, two instruments were being marked simultaneously. For example, measure 88 of the second movement of Quintet No. 2 has a "cres." under each instrument except the bassoon; since all upper instruments have the marking, the horn's notation was probably intended for the bassoon as well—or at least meant to imply a crescendo for the bassoon—thus avoiding any marks below the bassoon part which could potentially interfere with the next system in close spacing. While most dynamic markings are placed below the instrument line (as confirmed by the flute's markings), there are clear cases of placement above as well (e.g., Quintet No. 2, second movement, m. 93, where the "dolce" marking for the oboe is placed above the line while the *p* is below it; or Quintet No. 1, third movement, m. 93, where the "cres." marking placed between the horn and bassoon parts must refer to the bassoon since the horn is resting here). The horizontal placement of dynamic markings can also be ambiguous (see Quintet No. 2, first movement, mm. 7–8, where the markings for "cres." are placed rather haphazardly between four of the instruments—the clarinet's is actually written across the barline). The first movement of Quintet No. 1 displayed a few variants of the *sfz* marking between the horn and bassoon parts in measures 248 and 250; to achieve a similar effect between the instruments, the markings were transcribed as *sfz* (see critical notes).

Erasures

There are instances where material has been erased in the score. In most cases these would seem to make room for a correction or at least resolve the final intent of the composer and need no comment. The opening of Quintet No. 2, however, deserves special mention. Here, there is a tutti unison passage marked *f*. All instruments are given the same octave motive followed by a sixteenth, then step down to a whole note. Originally, the horn part seems to have had that written in for measure 1, but it has two erasures in beats 3–4 of that first measure, with the quarter note and quarter rest inked in (the original double dot of beat 3 can still be seen). The second measure has been left blank. It would seem, then, that Lachner's first intent was to have all five instruments play the motive, but later he decided to omit the horn after the initial octave drop. The quarter rest on beat 4 seems to make this later decision very clear, but the blank second measure (instead of a whole rest) leaves the issue somewhat open to question. The only other edition of the quintet (Monteux: Musica Rara, 1984) has the horn playing the entire two measures. The present edition inserts the passage in brackets, thus noting the issue, but ultimately allowing the performers to decide for themselves.

There are several instances where empty measures in a given instrument are not filled with rests but are left literally blank (e.g., Quintet No. 1, first movement, m. 9ff., bassoon part). While this might suggest potentially incomplete settings, it was more than likely simply an oversight saving time, so whole rests are added tacitly in the edition.

Pitches and Accidentals

All markings of the original concerning pitch have been conformed to modern practice; internal clarification of pitches (with letters) has not been noted, since the final (shown) intent is clear. In many cases, where there might be some ambiguity as to pitch, a cautionary accidental has been included by Lachner, who notates these as regular accidentals, i.e., without parentheses. Any instance of a cautionary accidental in the original that is not reflected in the edition has been reported in the critical notes. Lachner sometimes does use parentheses to enclose necessary accidentals as a "reminder" when the accidental repeats across a barline; in the edition, these parentheses have been removed but are mentioned in the critical notes. Editorially added accidentals fall into two categories: cautionary accidentals, which are placed in parentheses; and necessary accidentals deemed to be missing from the sources, which are placed in brackets.

Trills and Grace Notes

Trills are for the most part clearly marked in the quintets. The one movement of particular interest in this regard, however, is the third movement of Quintet No. 1, which features numerous trills throughout beginning in measure 52. While both the physical shape of the markings used in the manuscript and the context of their execution suggest the possibility of mordents, based on the markings used for trills elsewhere (on longer note values) they have been edited as trills, and performers will be able to decide, given a particular tempo, which is preferable.

Grace notes abound throughout Lachner's quintets. The problems they pose are obvious: because of their small size, pitches intended can at times be ambiguous. Moreover, clarification regarding accidentals is inconsistent. Thus, in Quintet No. 2, third movement, measure 9, the exit grace notes (*Nachschlag*) for the trill are unequally noted in the manuscript: all four instruments involved have a natural sign before the A, but only the oboe has a natural sign noted before the B, the others assuming one would carry the natural over from the trill note itself (an assumption held throughout the work and reflected in the modern edition).

Shortcuts

There are three major types of shortcuts used by Lachner in the quintets; all three are fairly standard procedures. One means of saving time is through the use of the ✗ sign, which is common and unproblematic. In these cases, a complete replicate of the given measure is made with the exception of dynamic markings, since these would be redundant in an immediately repeated measure.

Another time-saving device used by Lachner involves longer passages enclosed by a double set of repeat signs, ‖:‖. Unlike the former method, this approach involves all parts at once. The amount of material included within the repeat signs can vary from two measures to a longer section. Thus, in Quintet No. 2, fourth movement, measures 95–98 are enclosed by repeat signs and thus correspond to measures 99–102.

Finally, Lachner uses the terms "col flauto" and "octava." "Col flauto" is used in order to omit having to write the oboe part. In the present edition, all aspects of the flute part have been replicated including dynamic markings. "Octava" is used in the flute part to reduce the use of ledger lines. The practice is normal and unproblematic to edit; the present edition omits these references and displays the flute part in the octave intended. At times both terms are used in the oboe part, as in "col Flauto in 8va," in which case the flute part is replicated an octave lower.

Rhythmic Issues

For the most part, rhythmic interpretation did not present a real problem in the editorial process. Occasionally a dot would be missing, or the value of a grace note might be somewhat unclear, but generally, no major ambiguities, with one exception: the slashing of half notes to indicate eighth-note subdivision. While the practice itself is fairly common (indeed an accepted shortcut), carelessness in execution can lead to the "slash" becoming easily confused with a ledger line. Specific instances of problems in this regard were found in Quintet No 2. In the first movement in measure 194, the bassoon's half notes could be viewed as slashed (the markings seem at first too low for ledger lines), although the staccato half-note pattern lines up with the other three instruments playing and makes more sense in context. The flute part in measure 195 also appears confusing at first glance: the note initially seems to be a slashed half note, but it is really a half note whose stem is being deleted by a stroke to create a whole note (this type of deletion, or "correction," is obviously very confusing in this context, but understandable given the use of ink). One final example of rhythmic ambiguity occurs in the second movement, measure 37, where the bassoon part again makes it difficult to distinguish between a ledger line and a rhythmic stroke; once again, the context would seem to favor the former.

Corollary Material

This topic can be subdivided into two areas of concern: first, the presence of two distinct markings (ink and pencil); and second, the appearance of "sketches" on the bottom margins of some pages in the autograph manuscript.

There appears to be two types of entry: the original notation by Lachner in ink, and a secondary grainier entry in pencil, which corrects and revises. The latter entries, while distinguishable due to the lighter color, cannot be positively identified with the first hand: while it is possible (perhaps even probable) that Lachner made these revisions, the bigger and bulkier nature of these markings makes it harder to correlate them with complete certainty to the writing in ink. Nevertheless, since these later additions and alterations consistently clarify or correct mistakes and ambiguities of the original, they have been viewed as authoritative and final; thus, for the most part, no distinction was noted in their incorporation.

Some of the bottom staff systems of the score contain sketches, presumably working out harmonic and contrapuntal issues. This is especially evident in Quintet No. 2, beginning with page 7 of the first movement. The sketching appears on a single staff, stacking the instrument parts in a chord, and features the pencil (revisionist) writing. Moreover, the material does not necessarily correspond to the music on that given page, thus the intent of the sketches is not entirely clear. There are also several instances of major passages being crossed out and deleted throughout both quintets, in addition to numerous paste-overs; no attempt to record these was made, since the material left standing is assumed to be the final version.

Finally, as noted under "Sources," Quintet No. 1 contains two versions of the first two movements. Only the revised versions were used for the present edition, though references are made to the older versions in the following critical notes. One interesting difference between versions can be seen in the first movement, measure 21, where the older version has the flute continuing with the motive, while the revised version introduces the oboe here, followed by the flute in octaves—much more efective (compare plates 2 and 3). Notice also the working sketches apparent at the bottom of the original version.

Conflicting Material

The issue of conflicting material is often due to simple oversights, and these have generally been corrected via clear editorial indications or comments in the critical notes. There are other situations, however, that seem to conflict in a more subtle fashion, and these I have often left as is, assuming the performer will decide whether they want to alter an articulation or dynamic marking. A good example of this type of conflict can be found in Quintet No. 1, first movement, where the passage for flute beginning at measure 167 is non-staccato, but at its later appearance (m. 379) is clearly marked staccato. The discrepancy is obvious, but the ultimate intent of the composer, less so, therefore the passages were left as found in the manuscript.

Critical Notes

The critical notes below describe altered source readings not otherwise covered by the editorial method. The instruments are abbreviated as follows: Fl. = Flute; Ob. = Oboe; Cl. = Clarinet; Hn. = Horn; Bn. = Bassoon. The usual procedure of counting notes consecutively within a measure, grace notes included, has been adopted in the following, except in cases of notes included within a "slurred phrase," where notes are instead counted from the start of the slur to the end of the slur as shown in the edition, regardless of where in the measure the slur begins or how many measures it covers. Pitch names are standard: c′ refers to middle C.

Woodwind Quintet No. 1 in F Major

As noted above, there are two versions of movements 1 and 2 included in the manuscript. The following critical notes refer to the newer/revised versions unless otherwise noted.

[I] Andante; Allegro assai

Instrument specifications: "Flauto, Oboe, Clarinetto in B, Corno in F, Fagotto." First page has "1" marked in recto (upper right-hand corner). The older version has "Adagio" crossed out and replaced with the marking "Adante" [sic]. M. 1, Ob., slur is on notes 1–2; extended to m. 2, note 2 in edition. Mm. 5–7, Bn., slurred phrase has slurs on notes 2–4 and 4–7. Mm. 11–12, Hn., slurred phrase has slurs on notes 1–4 and 4–5. M. 12, Ob. and Cl. have crescendo hairpins; moved to m. 11 in edition. Mm. 13–14, Ob., slurred phrase has slurs on notes 1–3 and 3–4. Mm. 14–16, Ob., slurred phrase has slurs on notes 1–3 and 4–5. M. 15, Fl., slur is on notes 1–3; the slur has been extended to m. 16 in edition. M. 17, Hn., *p* noted at beginning of empty staff. Mm. 18–19, Bn., slurred phrase has slurs on notes 1–3 and 3–5. M. 19, Ob., note has cautionary ♮. Mm. 21–22, Ob., slurred phrase has slurs on notes 1–3, 3–4, and 4–6. M. 24, Bn., slur extends from note 3 to m. 25, note 8; extended to m. 26 in edition. M. 25, Hn., note 1 has *p*. M. 34, Cl., note 1 written as g′. M. 40, Cl., slur is on notes 2–3; extended to note 4 in edition. Mm. 45–47, Ob., slurs cover m. 45 and mm. 46–47; combined in edition. M. 47, Bn., slur goes to m. 48, note 5; extended to m. 49 in edition. M. 58, Fl., slur goes to note 1 of next measure. Mm. 63–64, Hn., slur goes to note 1 of m. 65. M. 81, Cl., note 1 has cautionary ♮. M. 101, Cl., note 1, ♯ is in parentheses. Mm. 107–10, Hn., slurred phrase has slurs on notes 1–5, 5–6, and 6–11. Mm. 108–9, Cl., slurred phrase has slurs on notes 1–2 and 2–3. Mm. 109–14, Bn., slurred phrase has slurs on notes 1–4 and 5–7. Mm. 113–15, Ob., slurred phrase has slurs on notes 1–5 and 6–10. M. 116, Ob., note 4, ♮ is in parentheses. Mm. 117–19, Fl. and Ob., slurred phrase has slurs on notes 1–5 and 6–10. Mm. 125–28, Ob., slurred phrase has slurs on notes 1–10 and 10–11. M. 133, "ritard" marked below the oboe, horn, and bassoon staves, but scratched out. Mm. 157–58, Ob., slur goes to note of m. 159. M. 161, Cl., slur goes to m. 162, note 2; extended to m. 163 in edition. M. 165, Fl., slur goes to note of next measure. M. 169, Cl., note 1 has *p*; moved to m. 168 in edition. M. 204, second ending has fermata on rest (for all instruments). M. 209, Cl., slur goes to note of next measure. M. 214, Cl., note 4 has cautionary ♮. M. 236, Cl., note 2 has cautionary ♯. M. 248, Hn., note 1, marking is possibly *fp* or *sfp*; changed to *sfz* in edition. M. 250, Hn., note 1 has *fs*; changed to *sfz* in edition. M. 252, Hn., note 1 is lacking. Mm. 255–58, Ob., slurred phrase has slurs on notes 1–3 and 3–9. M. 264, *p* marking on left margin, next to flute part. M. 267, Fl., slur goes to note 1 of next measure. M. 278, Cl., slur goes to m. 279, note 5; extended to m. 280 in edition. M. 290, Cl., note 1 has cautionary ♮. Mm. 317–19 and 325–27, Ob., slurred phrase has slurs on notes 1–5 and 6–10. M. 318, Ob., note 3 has staccato dot. M. 320, Bn., slur from note 2 goes to note of next measure. Mm. 321–23 and 329–31, Fl., slurred phrase has slurs on notes 1–5 and 6–10. M. 322, Fl., note 3 has staccato dot. M. 338, Ob., slur is on notes 1–6; it has been extended back to m. 337 in edition. M. 341, Fl., slur is on notes 1–5; extended back to m. 340 in edition. M. 345, "piu ritard" marked below the oboe staff, but crossed out. M. 346, Fl., quarter rest added at end of measure. M. 364, Bn., slur goes to note of next measure. M. 373, Bn., note 3 has cautionary ♮. M. 380, Bn., note 1 is d′, but see Fl., m. 388. M. 385, Ob., note 2 has cautionary ♮. M. 393, Ob., note 2 has cautionary ♮. M. 408, Fl., slur is on notes 2–3; extended to note 4 in edition.

[II] Scherzo: Allegro assai

The older version has a crossed-out alternate "Trio" section, followed by the revised one. M. 1, Cl., slur is on notes 1–2; extended to m. 2 in edition. M. 2, Cl., note 1 has staccato dot. M. 3, Ob. is marked "c[ol] Fl[auto] in 8va" (through m. 11, note 1). Mm. 7–9, Hn., slurred phrase has slurs on notes 1–3 and 3–7. Mm. 15–19, Ob., slurred phrase has slurs on notes 1–3 and 7–10. Mm. 15–16, Cl., slurred phrase has slurs on notes 1–7 and 7–8. Mm. 15–18, Hn., slurred phrase has slurs on notes 1–3 and 7–9 and is extended to note 10 (start of m. 19) in edition. M. 22, Fl., note has *p;* moved to m. 21 in edition. M. 23, "con fuoco" marking found in older version. M. 23, Ob. is marked "c[ol] Fl[auto] in 8" (through m. 50, note 1). M. 23, Ob., note 4 has cautionary ♭. M. 25, Ob., slur goes to note 1 of next measure. M. 33, Bn., slur is on notes 2–3; extended to note 4 in edition. M. 33, Bn., note 5 has cautionary ♯. M. 48, Bn., slur goes to note 4. M. 56, Ob. is marked "c[ol] Fl[auto] in 8" (through end of movement). Mm. 80–81, Cl., slurred phrase has slurs on notes 1–2 and 3–5. M. 89, "Da Capo" is written very lightly above a "Dal Segno il Fine" indication; since the movement does not contain a segno anywhere (nor does the first, older version), and in light of the typical repeat format for these movements, the "Da Capo" indication has been retained, which takes one back to the very beginning, and then to the "Fine," as indicated.

[III] ANDANTE; ALLEGRO; ANDANTE

Anacrusis to m. 1, Ob., slurred phrase has slurs on notes 2–3 and 4–7. Mm. 2–3, Fl., slurred phrase has slurs on notes 1–3 and 4–5. Mm. 2–3, Cl., slurred phrase has slurs on notes 1–2 and 2–5. Mm. 9–10 and 12–13, Fl., slurred phrase has slurs on notes 2–3 and 4–7. M. 9, Hn., slurred phrase has slurs on notes 1–2 and 3–6 (it appears that a single slur was originally in source but was then erased). Mm. 14–15, Ob., slurred phrase has slurs on notes 1–2 and 2–3. Mm. 20–21, Ob., slurred phrase has slurs on notes 1–3 and 4–7. Mm. 21–22, Cl., slurred phrase has slurs on notes 1–2 and 3–6. Mm. 22–23, Fl., slurred phrase has slurs on notes 1–3 and 4–5. Mm. 22–23, Bn., slurred phrase has slurs on notes 1–2 and 2–3. Mm. 26–27, Cl., slurred phrase has slurs on notes 1–2 and 2–6. Mm. 26–27, Bn., slurred phrase has slurs on notes 1–2 and 2–3. Mm. 27–28, Bn., slurred phrase has slurs on notes 1–4 and 5–8. Mm. 32–33, Fl., slurred phrase has slurs on notes 1–2 and 2–3. Mm. 32–33, Hn., slurred phrase has slurs on notes 1–2 and 2–3. Mm. 33–35, Cl., slurred phrase has slurs on notes 2–3 and 4–8. Mm. 34–35, Hn., slurred phrase has slurs on notes 1–2 and 3–5. M. 40, Cl., note 1 could be written as g'. M. 41, Ob., note has cautionary ♭. Mm. 42–44, Fl., slurred phrase has slurs on notes 1–3 and 4–7. Mm. 43–44, Ob., slurred phrase has slurs on notes 1–2 and 3–6. M. 43, Cl., slurred phrase has slurs on notes 1–2 and 3–6. Mm. 53–60, the repetition of these bars is written out in the edition as mm. 73–80; see introduction under "Lachner's Quintets." M. 53 has segno ("#") and "sempre staccato" indication; the latter moved to m. 55 in edition. M. 53, Fl., slur is on notes 1–2; extended back to m. 52 in edition. M. 55, Fl., slur is on notes 1–2; extended back to m. 54 in edition. M. 59, Cl., slur is on notes 1–2; extended back to m. 58 in edition. M. 61, Ob., slur is on notes 1–2; extended back to m. 60 in edition. M. 61, Hn., slur is on notes 5–6; extended back to note 2 in edition. M. 63, Cl., slur is on notes 1–2; extended back to m. 62 in edition. M. 69, Cl., note 1 has *p;* moved to m. 68 in edition. M. 72 has "Dal # il Fine." M. 80, "Piu mosso" title scratched out and replaced with "Allegro." M. 89, Ob., note 4 has staccato dot. M. 94, Hn., note has cautionary ♭. M. 96, Hn., note 3 has cautionary ♭. M. 102, Cl., note has cautionary ♭. Mm. 107–8, Hn., slurred phrase has slurs on notes 1–2 and 2–3. Mm. 107–8, Bn., slurred phrase has slurs on notes 1–4 and 4–5. M. 112, originally a second ending, but first ending crossed out. M. 119, Ob., note 2 has cautionary ♮. M. 125, Fl., note 1 has *p.* Mm. 125–26, Bn., slurred phrase has slurs on notes 1–2 and 2–3. M. 138, Hn., rest has *dim.* indication. Mm. 139–40, Hn., slurred phrase has slurs on notes 2–3 and 4–7. M. 145, "ritard" marked below the flute and horn staves, but scratched out. M. 146, Hn., note 1 is notated in bass clef; the bass clef has been moved to beat 2 in the edition. M. 147, final barline is thin-thin.

[IV] ALLEGRO

"Vivace" is marked next to "Allegro" but is scratched out. M. 1, Cl., note 2, accent is written vertically. Mm. 19–20, Cl., slur goes to note 1 of m. 21. M. 25, Ob., note has cautionary ♮. M. 28, Bn., slur goes to note of next measure. M. 29, Ob., slur goes from note 2 to note 1 of next measure. M. 30, Bn., slur goes to note 1 of next measure. M. 46, Ob., slur goes from note 2 to note 1 of next measure. M. 50, Ob., slur goes to note 1 of next measure. M. 55, Cl., notes 5–6 have staccato dots; slur substituted in edition to match Ob. and Bn. M. 63, Ob. marked "col Flauto in 8va" (through m. 76). M. 71, Hn., slur goes to note of next measure. M. 72, Bn., note 1 has cautionary ♮. M. 76, Fl. and Ob., slur is on notes 1–4; extended back to m. 75 in edition. M. 77, "ritard" marked below the flute, oboe, and horn staves; set as score instruction in edition. M. 79, Cl., note has cautionary ♮. M. 93, Fl., note 1 has staccato dot. M. 98, Hn., note 1 has ♯; moved to note 2 in edition. M. 99, Ob., note 6 has cautionary ♮. M. 108, Hn., note has ♭. M. 128, Ob., note 3, accent is written vertically. Mm. 129–58, only flute part is written out; all other parts are indicated "ut supra" and measures are numbered (m. 129 = 1), which implies repetition of the beginning of the work, so that m. 129 = m. 2 and so forth, to m. 159 (= m. 32), where all parts are written out once again. Mm. 169–70, Fl., slurred phrase has slurs on notes 1–2 and 2–4. M. 182, Ob., note 6 has cautionary ♯. Mm. 186–87, Cl. and Hn., slurred phrase has slurs on notes 1–2 and 2–3. M. 206, Fl., note 1 written as whole note. M. 207, "ritard" marked below the flute and clarinet staves; set as score instruction in edition. M. 227, Ob., slur goes to note 1 of next measure. M. 237, Fl., slur goes to note of next measure. M. 239, Fl., slur goes to note of next measure. Mm. 245–46, Fl., slur goes to note of m. 247. Mm. 245–46, Cl., slur (extended back to enclose ties in edition) goes to note 1 of m. 247. M. 246, Ob., slur goes to note of next measure. M. 247, "Piu mosso" marked below the flute, oboe, and horn staves.

M. 248, Fl. and Ob., slur goes to note of next measure. M. 250, Fl. and Ob., slur goes to note 1 of next measure. M. 254, Fl. and Ob., slur goes to note of next measure. M. 256, Ob., slur goes to note 1 of next measure. M. 258, Bn., slur goes to note 1 of next measure. M. 259, all instruments, slur goes to note 1 of next measure. M. 260, Fl. and Ob., slur goes to note 1 of next measure. M. 261, all instruments, slur goes to note 1 of next measure.

Woodwind Quintet No. 2 in E-flat Major

[I] Allegro

Instrument specifications: "Flauto, Oboe, Clarinetto in B, Corno in Es, Fagotto" ("Fagot" originally written in horn staff, but crossed out, replaced with "Corno"). M. 1, Hn., note 2, double augmentation dot erased, and beat 3 has quarter rest. Mm. 3 and 5, Fl., note 2, double augmentation dot missing. Mm. 11–13, Ob., slurred phrase has slurs on notes 1–5 and 5–9. M. 11, Cl., slur extends from note 7 to m. 12, note 1; extended to m. 13 in edition. M. 17, Fl., slurred phrase has slurs on notes 1–5 and 5–6. M. 26, Cl., note 1 written as dotted quarter note. M. 33, Bn., note has cautionary ♭. M. 45, Ob., note 2 has *p;* changed to *fp* in edition (see m. 207). Mm. 45–47, Ob., slurred phrase has slurs on notes 1–2 and 2–3. M. 46, Cl. and Bn., note has *p*. M. 65, Cl., slurred phrase has slurs on notes 1–5 and 6–9. M. 71, Fl., slur is on notes 1–4; curtailed to end on note 3 in edition. M. 71, Bn., slurred phrase has slurs on notes 1–9 and 9–16. M. 83, Hn., note 4, entered twice, first time crossed out. M. 84, Hn., single slur covers whole measure. M. 90, Hn., note 1 written as quarter note. M. 92, Ob., slur is on notes 2–3; extended to m. 93 in edition. M. 98, all staves, repeat at beginning/end of measure implies repetition of only that measure (= m. 99). M. 100, Cl., single slur covers whole measure. Mm. 111 and 113, Ob., note 1, added in pencil (over inked quarter rest). M. 111, Cl., note 8 has cautionary ♭. M. 117, Fl. and Hn., slur is on notes 2–4; extended back to note 1 in edition. M. 120, Hn., single slur extends from note 1 to m. 121, note 3. M. 122, Hn., slur is on notes 1–4; extended back to m. 121 in edition. M. 149, Ob., single slur covers whole measure. Mm. 153–54, Bn., slurred phrase has slurs on notes 1–2 and 3–4. M. 154, Fl., note 2 has slur to m. 155. M. 154, Bn., note 2 and following rest written in pencil. M. 156, Cl., note 2, double augmentation dot missing. Mm. 157–58, Bn., notes originally an octave higher. M. 171, Fl., note 2 has *p*. M. 172, Cl., note 1 has *f*. M. 193, Ob., *pp* dynamic crossed out. M. 196, Bn. has crescendo hairpin; moved to m. 195 in edition. M. 204, Bn., slur begins on note 2; moved to begin on note 1 in edition. M. 208, Fl., slur from note 2 goes to note 1 of next measure. M. 210, Hn., slur goes to note 1 of next measure. M. 221, Ob., note has *fp;* changed to *f* in edition. M. 229, clarinet moves to second staff in system, oboe moves to third (all staves but flute relabeled). M. 233, oboe and clarinet switch back to original locations on staff system. M. 239, Fl. has slur covering whole measure. M. 240, Fl. has slur covering whole measure. M. 253, Hn., slur is on notes 1–2; extended to m. 254 in edition. M. 255, Ob., slur is on notes 1–2; extended to note 3 in edition. M. 255, Hn., slur is on notes 2–3; extended to m. 256 in edition. M. 257, horn and clarinet switch positions on staff sytem. M. 261, horn and clarinet switch back, but not marked. M. 261, Cl. has slur covering notes 2–9. M. 286, Ob., slur goes to note 1 of next measure. M. 295, Hn., note written as quarter note.

[II] Andante con moto

Horn part has "in Es" reminder at beginning of movement to the left of the staff. Mm. 21–24, Bn., slurred phrase has slurs on notes 1–7 and 7–10. M. 27, Ob., note 2 has cautionary ♭. M. 28, Fl., *pp* dynamic added in pencil. M. 71, Bn., slur goes to note 1 of next measure. M. 86, Cl., note 4 has cautionary ♮. M. 91, Ob., slur goes to note 1 of next measure. M. 93, Hn., *pp* dynamic added in pencil. Mm. 101 and 103, Bn., augmentation dot missing. Mm. 113–14, Fl., slurred phrase has slurs on notes 1–5 and 5–7. M. 116, Fl., note 4 has cautionary ♯. Mm. 121–26, indication for 8th-note subdivision crossed out in both oboe and horn parts (pencil). Mm. 149–50, Fl., slur goes to m. 150, note 3. M. 151, all instruments, *pp* dynamic added in pencil. M. 160, Fl., slur is on notes 2–4; curtailed to begin on note 3 in edition. M. 164, Hn., end of measure has decrescendo hairpin; moved to m. 165 in edition. Mm. 179–81, indication for 8th-note subdivision crossed out in both oboe and horn parts (pencil). Mm. 197–98, Ob., single slur covers both measures. M. 199, Cl., slur is on notes 2–6; extended back to note 1 in edition. M. 217, Ob., notes 2–3 (grace notes) have cautionary ♮ and ♭, respectively. Mm. 219–24, indication for 8th-note subdivision crossed out in both flute and clarinet parts (pencil). Mm. 229 and 230, Cl., beat 3 is marked by "3". M. 234, Cl., beat 2 is marked by "3".

[III] Menuetto: Allegro assai

Last page of second movement has "Menuetto" at the bottom; first page of third movement has "Menetto" [*sic*] at the top. M. 9, Ob., note 3 (second grace note) has cautionary ♮. Mm. 12–14, Ob., slurred phrase has slurs on notes 1–2 and 2–7. Mm. 13–14, Fl., slur covers both measures; extended back to m. 12 in edition. M. 47, Bn., slur extends from note 2 to m. 48, note 1; extended back to m. 46 in edition. M. 81, beat 3, "Trio" section re-enters key and time signatures. M. 119, Fl. and Ob., slur is on notes 1–2; extended to m. 120, note 3 in edition. Mm. 121 and 125, Fl., Ob., Cl., and Bn., septuplet notes are 32d notes. M. 128, Cl., note 2 has cautionary ♮. Mm. 152–53, Fl. and Ob., slurred phrase has slurs on notes 1–5 and 5–6. M. 173 has "Menuetto da capo il Fine." M. 173, final barline is a repeat bar.

[IV] Allegretto

M. 6, Cl., *p* dynamic added in pencil. M. 10, Fl., note 3 has stroke; changed to accent in edition. M. 17, Ob., slur is on notes 2–4; extended back to encompass tie and forward to m. 18, note 3 in edition. Mm. 23–24, Hn., *fz* markings added in pencil. M. 31, Ob., *fz* marking added in pencil. Mm. 31–32, Hn., *fz* markings added in pencil. M. 34, Ob., note 3, augmentation dot missing. M. 35, Cl., second slur is on notes 3–4; extended to m. 36 in edition. M. 36, Fl., slur is on notes 1–6; extended back to m. 35 in edition. M. 40, Fl., slurred phrase has slurs on notes 1–3 and 4–6. M. 45, Fl., Ob., and Cl., "dim" marking added in pencil. M. 56, Ob., note 3 has cautionary ♮. M. 67, Ob., note 2, augmentation dot missing. M. 85, Ob., note 2, augmentation dot missing. M. 85, Cl., note 4, augmentation dot missing. M. 95, Bn., note 8, augmentation dot missing. M. 98, Ob., note 2, augmentation dot missing. M. 110, Bn., note 4 has f; moved to note 2 in edition. Mm. 126 and 127, Fl., slurred phrase has slurs on notes 1–2 and 3–5. Mm. 130 and 131, Ob., slurred phrase has slurs on notes 1–2 and 3–5. M. 133, Cl., slurred phrase has slurs on notes 1–2 and 3–5. Mm. 134 and 135, Cl., slur is on notes 1–2; extended to note 5 in edition. M. 137, Fl. and Cl., slurred phrase has slurs on notes 1–2 and 3–5. M. 168, Ob., slur is on notes 1–4; extended to note 5 in edition. Mm. 168–69, Cl., slurred phrase has slurs on notes 1–3 and 4–5. Mm. 177–78, Bn., slurred phrase has slurs on notes 1–6 and 6–9. Mm. 179–80, Ob., slurred phrase has slurs on notes 2–4 and 5–8. Mm. 188–91, Bn., slurred phrase has slurs on notes 1–3 and 3–8. M. 203, Ob., note 1 has cautionary ♭. M. 205, Fl., slurs are on notes 1–3 and 4–6; combined and extended back to m. 204 in edition. Mm. 206–7, Fl., slurred phrase has slurs on notes 1–2 and 3–8 and is extended to note 9 (start of m. 208) in edition. Mm. 208–9, Ob. and Cl., slurred phrase has slurs on notes 1–2 and 3–8. Mm. 210–11, Ob., slurred phrase has slurs on notes 1–2 and 3–8. M. 254, Cl. has p dynamic in second half of measure (under the rests). Mm. 256–58, Hn. and Bn., slurred phrase has slurs on notes 1–2 and 2–4. M. 261, Bn., single slur covers whole measure; slur on notes 4–5 added in what appears to be pencil. Mm. 261–63, Bn., strokes added in what appears to be pencil. Mm. 262 and 263, Bn., single slur covers whole measure; slurs on notes 1–2 and 4–5 added in what appears to be pencil. M. 264, Bn., slur on notes 1–2 added in what appears to be pencil. M. 265, Bn., two slurs in measure, each covering three notes. M. 309, Bn., one extra 8th rest in measure. [M. 313], an extra empty measure is added at the end (with fermata in flute part).

RECENT RESEARCHES IN THE MUSIC OF THE NINETEENTH AND
EARLY TWENTIETH CENTURIES
Rufus Hallmark, general editor

Vol.	Composer: Title
1–2	Jan Ladislav Dussek: *Selected Piano Works*
3–4	Johann Nepomuk Hummel: *Piano Concerto, Opus 113*
5	*One Hundred Years of Eichendorff Songs*
6	Etienne-Nicolas Méhul: *Symphony No. 1 in G Minor*
7–8	*Embellished Opera Arias*
9	*The Nineteenth-Century Piano Ballade: An Anthology*
10	*Famous Poets, Neglected Composers: Songs to Lyrics by Goethe, Heine, Mörike, and Others*
11	Charles-Marie Widor: *The Symphonies for Organ: Symphonie I*
12	Charles-Marie Widor: *The Symphonies for Organ: Symphonie II*
13	Charles-Marie Widor: *The Symphonies for Organ: Symphonie III*
14	Charles-Marie Widor: *The Symphonies for Organ: Symphonie IV*
15	Charles-Marie Widor: *The Symphonies for Organ: Symphonie V*
16	Charles-Marie Widor: *The Symphonies for Organ: Symphonie VI*
17	Charles-Marie Widor: *The Symphonies for Organ: Symphonie VII*
18	Charles-Marie Widor: *The Symphonies for Organ: Symphonie VIII*
19	Charles-Marie Widor: *The Symphonies for Organ: Symphonie gothique*
20	Charles-Marie Widor: *The Symphonies for Organ: Symphonie romane*
21	Archduke Rudolph of Austria: *Forty Variations on a Theme by Beethoven for Piano; Sonata in F Minor for Violin and Piano*
22	Fanny Hensel: *Songs for Pianoforte, 1836–1837*
23	*Anthology of Goethe Songs*
24	Walter Rabl: *Complete Instrumental Chamber Works*
25	Stefano Pavesi: *Dies irae concertato*
26	Franz Liszt: *St. Stanislaus: Scene 1, Two Polonaises, Scene 4*
27	George Frederick Pinto: *Three Sonatas for Pianoforte with Violin*
28	Felix Mendelssohn: *Concerto for Two Pianos and Orchestra in E Major (1823): Original Version of the First Movement*
29	Johann Nepomuk Hummel: *Mozart's* Haffner *and* Linz *Symphonies*
30–31	Gustav Mahler: *Die drei Pintos: Based on Sketches and Original Music of Carl Maria von Weber*
32	Niels W. Gade: *St. Hans' Evening Play Overture*
33	Charles-Marie Widor: *Symphonie pour orgue et orchestre, opus 42bis*
34	Edvard Grieg: *The Unfinished Chamber Music*

35	Johann Nepomuk Hummel: *Twelve Select Overtures*
36	*Motets for One Voice by Franck, Gounod, and Saint-Saëns*
37	*Topical Song Cycles of the Early Nineteenth Century*
38	Alice Mary Smith: *Symphonies*
39	Franz Lachner: *Two Woodwind Quintets*

CHECK FOR 10 PARTS